Systematic Reviews and Meta-Analysis

P O C K E T   G U I D E S   T O
SOCIAL WORK RESEARCH METHODS

Series Editor
Tony Tripodi, DSW
Professor Emeritus, Ohio State University

Determining Sample Size
Balancing Power, Precision, and Practicality
Patrick Dattalo

Preparing Research Articles
Bruce A. Thyer

JULIA H. LITTELL
JACQUELINE CORCORAN
VIJAYAN PILLAI

Systematic Reviews
and
Meta-Analysis

OXFORD
UNIVERSITY PRESS

2008

OXFORD
UNIVERSITY PRESS

Oxford University Press, Inc., publishes works that further
Oxford University's objective of excellence
in research, scholarship, and education.

Oxford   New York
Auckland   Cape Town   Dar es Salaam   Hong Kong   Karachi
Kuala Lumpur   Madrid   Melbourne   Mexico City   Nairobi
New Delhi   Shanghai   Taipei   Toronto

With offices in
Argentina   Austria   Brazil   Chile   Czech Republic   France   Greece
Guatemala   Hungary   Italy   Japan   Poland   Portugal   Singapore
South Korea   Switzerland   Thailand   Turkey   Ukraine   Vietnam

Published by Oxford University Press, Inc.
198 Madison Avenue, New York, New York 10016

www.oup.com

Oxford is a registered trademark of Oxford University Press

Library of Congress Cataloging-in-Publication Data
Littell, Julia H.
Systematic reviews and meta-analysis / Julia H. Littell, Jacqueline
Corcoran, and Vijayan Pillai.
p. cm.—(Pocket guides to social work research methods)
Includes bibliographical references and index.
ISBN 978-0-19-532654-3 (pbk. : alk. paper)   1. Social
sciences—Research—Evaluation.   2. Meta-analysis.   I. Corcoran,
Jacqueline.   II. Pillai, Vijayan K.   III. Title.
H62.L494 2008
001.4'2—dc22   2007041604

1 3 5 7 9 8 6 4 2

Printed in the United States of America
on acid-free paper

Table of Contents

Systematic Reviews and Meta-Analysis

1

Introduction

Systematic reviews and meta-analysis are distinct but highly compatible approaches to research synthesis. When used in tandem, these methods embody a scientific approach to the identification, analysis, and synthesis of quantitative evidence from previous studies. They can be used to summarize large bodies of research and generate new insights for social work and social policy.

A *systematic review* aims to comprehensively locate and synthesize research that bears on a particular question, using organized, transparent, and replicable procedures at each step in the process. Good systematic reviews take ample precautions to minimize error and bias. This is particularly important in research synthesis, because biases can arise in the original studies as well as in publication, dissemination, and review processes, and these biases can be cumulative. Bias consistently exaggerates or underestimates effects, and it can lead to wrong conclusions. Like any good study, a systematic review follows a protocol (a detailed plan) that specifies its central objectives, concepts, and methods in advance. Steps and decisions are carefully documented so that readers can follow and evaluate reviewers' methods (Moher et al., 1999; Sutton et al., 1998). *Meta-analysis* is a set of statistical methods for combining quantitative results from multiple studies to produce an overall

summary of empirical knowledge on a given topic. It is used to analyze central trends and variations in results across studies, and to correct for error and bias in a body of research. Results of the original
studies usually are converted to one or more common metrics, called
effect sizes, which are then combined across studies. This allows us to
synthesize results from studies that use different measures of the same
construct or report results in different ways.

The terms *systematic review* and *meta-analysis* are not synonymous.
Many published meta-analyses are not systematic reviews. Meta-analysis
can (and should) be embedded in a systematic review, but this is not
always done. Some systematic reviews employ other synthesis methods
or provide no synthesis at all. For example, the Cochrane Collaboration
(described further on) publishes "empty" reviews. These reviews are
systematic because they were conducted according to plans described
in a published protocol, but reviewers found no studies that met the
criteria for the review. (Such "empty" reviews can be useful to policy
makers who decide where investments in primary research are needed.)
A single systematic review can contain multiple meta-analyses, including separate analyses of effects on different outcomes, as well as the use
of a variety of meta-analytic techniques.

Systematic review methods are not new, nor did they originate in the
biomedical sciences. Early systematic research syntheses can be found in
education and psychology (Chalmers, Hedges, & Cooper, 2002; Petticrew & Roberts, 2006). Meta-analysis may have begun with Karl Pearson's 1904 synthesis of results from several studies of a vaccine against
typhoid. After a long period of dormancy, meta-analysis captured the
interest of social and behavioral scientists in the late 1970s, when Gene
Glass (1976) coined the term and several teams used statistical methods
to synthesize results from many studies of the effects of psychotherapy
(Smith & Glass, 1977), effects of classroom size on achievement (Glass &
Smith, 1978), interpersonal expectancy effects (Rosenthal & Rubin,
1979), and the validity of employment tests based on race (Hunter,
Schmidt, & Hunter, 1979).

In the mid-1980s, Light and Pillemer (1984) described a general,
scientific approach to synthesizing research for social policy. Hedges

and Olkin (1985) and others developed statistical methods for meta-analysis. Following the publication of the first edition of the *Handbook of Research Synthesis* (Cooper & Hedges, 1994) and other texts on the science of research synthesis (Cooper, 1998), meta-analysis evolved into a set of statistical techniques that can be embedded in systematic reviews to minimize bias.

In social work, interest in research synthesis was sparked by Fischer's (1973) controversial review, "Is Casework Effective?" The 1980s and 1990s saw a growing interest in meta-analysis among social work researchers (De Smidt & Gorey, 1997; Fischer, 1990; Fraser, Nelson, & Rivard, 1997; Gorey, Thyer, & Pawluck, 1998; Grenier & Gorey, 1998; Holden, 1991; Videka-Sherman, 1988). In the past decade, a few social work scholars have been active in the international interdisciplinary organizations that develop standards for meta-analysis and systematic reviews of empirical research in the social, behavioral, and health sciences.

The number of systematic reviews and meta-analytic studies has burgeoned since the mid-1990s. Much of this work has occurred in the health sciences. A recent sample of reviews indexed in MEDLINE shows that systematic reviews are produced at the rate of about 2,500 a year (Moher et al., 2007). Online searches will produce over 10,000 hits for "systematic review" and 27,000 hits for "meta-analysis" in MEDLINE/PubMed. The same queries return approximately 1,800 hits for systematic reviews (SR) and 6,800 for meta-analysis (MA) in PsycINFO; 400 (SR) and 1,600 (MA) in Sociological Abstracts; and 22 (SR) and 85 (MA) in Social Work Abstracts. While these databases vary in size (PubMed has almost 2 million records, PsycINFO has 1.4 million, Social Work Abstracts has 34,000) and social work scholars have published meta-analyses that appear in other databases (including PubMed, Psyc-INFO, and the Cochrane Database of Systematic Reviews), a recent study suggests that social work lags behind allied disciplines (psychology, psychiatry, and nursing) in its adoption of meta-analysis as a research methodology and in critical appraisal of published meta-analyses (Lundahl & Yaffe, 2007).

The recent interest in research synthesis in the social, behavioral, and health sciences is closely related to the movement toward evidence-based practice. This began in medicine in the early 1990s (Sackett et al., 1991) and has become prominent in all of the helping professions. Evidence-based practice was defined by Sackett (2000) and colleagues as the integration of the best available research knowledge with clinical expertise and consumer values. In evidence-based practice, the clinician evaluates the appropriateness of a certain approach for a particular consumer's condition and context by considering relevant information that includes the results of treatment outcome studies (Gibbs, 2003). This approach reflects social work's long-standing interest in using scientific information to advance ethical practice and policy (Gambrill, 2006; Gibbs & Gambrill, 2002; Zimbalist, 1977). The evidence-based practice movement also reflects increased emphasis on accountability to consumers (clients) and third-party payers, such as insurance companies and government agencies, and the desire to extend the knowledge base of the helping professions.

To keep up with research in this field, readers must locate relevant studies, assess their credibility, and integrate credible results with findings from previous studies. This has become increasingly difficult as research findings and other information have accumulated rapidly. The synthesis of empirical evidence is further complicated by the fact that credible studies may use different research designs, include different types of participants, employ different measures, and produce inconsistent results. Systematic reviews carefully document and appraise study qualities, while meta-analyses provide quantitative summaries of evidence, showing the central trends, variations, and possible reasons for differences in results across studies. Hence, these reviews can provide new insights about the evidence that is relevant for social work and social policy. Indeed, systematic reviews and meta-analysis are becoming more widely used in the social sciences, especially in psychology and education, and have been adopted as the standard for synthesizing results of clinical trials in medicine. These methods are also being used to synthesize the enormous body of human genome research, along with epidemiological data and studies of risk factors.

We will show that systematic reviews and meta-analysis have distinct advantages over other qualitative and quantitative approaches to synthesizing research for policy and practice. We will also discuss their limitations. First, though, it is important to dispel some myths about these methods.

As shown in Table 1.1, misunderstandings about systematic reviews and meta-analysis abound. These are sometimes viewed as a very narrow set of tools, more appropriate for "simple" biomedical research than for the complex interventions of the helping professions. But this is a false

Table 1.1. Myths about Systematic Reviews and Meta-Analysis

Myth	Fact
Meta-analysis comes from biomedical research and requires a medical perspective.	Meta-analysis was initially developed in the social and behavioral sciences and is widely used outside of medicine.
Systematic reviews and meta-analyses are appropriate only for studies of treatment effects.	These methods are appropriate for many kinds of research questions. Meta-analysis is used to synthesize research on correlations, epidemiological data (incidence and prevalence rates), accuracy of diagnostic tests, prognostic accuracy (etiological and risk factors), and treatment effects.
Systematic reviews can (or should) include only randomized controlled trials (RCTs).	Many systematic reviews include nonrandomized designs, such as case-control studies, interrupted time-series designs, prospective before-and-after design, nonequivalent comparison groups (often with matching), and RCTs. The research question dictates appropriate designs.
Meta-analysis requires many studies.	Meta-analysis can be performed with two studies.
Meta-analysis requires large studies.	Sample size in the original studies is not an appropriate inclusion criterion. There are tests and corrections for small-sample bias. Meta-analysis can be used with single-subject designs (also known as individual patient data [IPD]).
Meta-analysis can overcome problems with quality (validity) in original studies.	Study qualities can be examined, analyses can detect which study qualities may matter, and results of higher-quality studies can be emphasized. Meta-analysis does not improve the quality of original studies ("garbage in, garbage out").

dichotomy: biomedical research is not simple. There is a large body of medical research on complex biopsychosocial interventions and strategies to improve the quality of health care (from efforts to promote hand washing in hospitals to elaborate financing schemes). Concerns about adherence to prescribed regimens are akin to concerns about fidelity to psychosocial treatments in social services. Complex interaction effects arise in many drug trials, just as they do in studies of social and behavioral interventions.

Throughout this book we will confront misunderstandings about systematic reviews and meta-analyses. However, as the last item in Table 1.1 suggests, it is important to note that these methods of research synthesis are not alchemical: they do not turn lead (i.e., poor-quality studies) into gold.

Appropriate Topics

Systematic reviews can be used to address many different kinds of research questions, and meta-analysis can combine different forms of quantitative data. Suitable topics for systematic reviews and meta-analyses include inquiries about the central tendency or distribution of values of a single variable, the direction and strength of associations between two variables, effects of interventions, interactions among variables (e.g., differential effects), and so forth. To appreciate the diverse range of topics and questions that can be covered, consider the following illustrations.

Univariate proportions or averages can be derived from multiple studies and then weighted (usually by sample size or precision) to generate pooled estimates. For example, Ahnert, Pinquart, and Lamb (2006) synthesized results from 40 studies to estimate the proportions of children who had secure attachments to their parents (>60%) and to nonparental day-care providers (42%). The investigators also assessed factors associated with secure attachment to day-care providers.

Correlational data can be synthesized to investigate the strength of associations between variables. This approach has been used in meta-analyses of the associations between attitudes and behavior (Glasman & Albarracin, 2006), sensation-seeking and alcohol use (Hittner & Swickert, 2006), interpersonal stress and psychosocial health in children and adolescents (Clarke, 2006), self-reported intimate-partner violence and social-desirability bias (Sugarman & Hotaling, 1997), and factors associated with turnover and retention in human services (Barak, Nissly, & Levin, 2001).

Many systematic reviews and meta-analyses summarize results of previous studies of intervention effects. Several thousand systematic reviews and meta-analyses have been conducted on effects of social, behavioral, educational, and medical interventions. Contrary to popular misconceptions, meta-analyses can synthesize studies of complex, multicomponent interventions, as well as "simpler" drug trials. Sometimes the results of these meta-analyses are surprising. A systematic review and meta-analysis by Petrosino, Turpin-Petrosino, and Buehler (2003) shows that Scared Straight programs intended to frighten juveniles and thus turn them away from criminal activity actually have opposite effects. Littell, Popa, and Forsythe's (2005) review shows that the effects of a prominent model program, Multisystemic Therapy, are inconsistent across studies—a finding that contradicts dozens of traditional, narrative reviews on this topic (Littell, in press).

In addition to assessing main effects of treatments, meta-analysis can be used to assess the extent to which effects vary and to explore possible explanations for variations. For example, in a systematic review and meta-analysis of interventions that were intended to reduce unplanned teenage pregnancies, Scher and colleagues (Scher, Maynard, & Stagner, 2006) produced separate estimates of effects for different types of programs (see Fig. 1.1). For ease of interpretation, pregnancy risks were reported as percentages, and the treatment effect is understood as a reduction (or increase) in the percentage of youth who are likely to experience pregnancy. These authors also reported results by gender, for different age groups, and for different types of studies (randomized experiments versus nonrandomized studies).

Using data from many studies, meta-analysts can address some questions that were not (and perhaps could not have been) considered

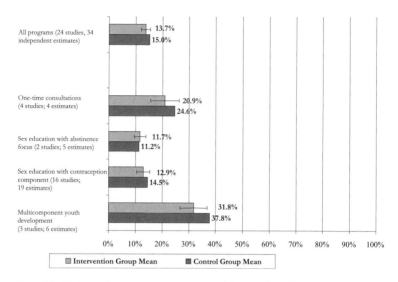

Figure 1.1. Estimated impacts on pregnancy risk rates for all programs, and by program type. *Source*: Scher, Maynard, & Stagner, 2006.

in the original studies. By capitalizing on between-study variations in sample and treatment characteristics, meta-analysis can explore potential moderators of treatment effects to assess whether treatments are more or less effective with different kinds of cases (e.g., older or younger children), in different doses (longer- or shorter-term treatment), and under different circumstances. Wilson, Lipsey, and Soydan (2003) found that mainstream programs for juvenile delinquency are as effective for minority youth as they are for majority youth. Shadish and colleagues showed that the research setting (university or agency) is confounded with several other variables, but when the influence of those variables is controlled, effects of psychotherapy are robust across conditions, from university clinics to clinically representative settings (Shadish, Matt, Navarro, & Phillips, 2000). Meta-analysis has been used to synthesize information on the accuracy of diagnostic tests and the prognostic performance of tests. For example, Stone and colleagues (2005) synthesized data on the misdiagnosis of conversion symptoms and "hysteria." Shlonsky and Saini (2005) have begun a systematic review and meta-analysis of the predictive validity of instruments that aim to assess the risk of recurrence of child maltreatment. Statistical models for meta-analysis of studies of diagnostic and prognostic tests are under development (Altman, 2001).

Petticrew (2001) cited systematic reviews and meta-analyses that showed the following:

- Resource investments in schools are positively related to student outcomes (Hedges, Laine, & Greenwald, 1994).
- Men and women are equally effective in leadership and managerial roles (Eagly, Karau, & Makhijani, 1995).
- There are no discernible differences between homosexual and heterosexual parents in terms of their parenting styles or of the emotional adjustment and sexual orientation of their children (Allen & Burrell, 1996).
- Jurors' sentencing decisions are influenced by defendants' race (Sweeney & Haney, 1992).

The following are the results of more recent systematic reviews and meta-analyses:

- Structured volunteer tutoring improves students' reading and language skills (Ritter et al., 2006).
- Social information processing interventions reduce aggressive and disruptive behavior in school-age children (Wilson & Lipsey, 2006a, 2006b).
- Sex education programs do not have consistent effects on teenagers' sexual behavior, but abstinence-focused programs appear to increase pregnancy rates (Scher, Maynard, & Stagner, 2006).
- Mass media campaigns to promote HIV testing have immediate, positive effects (Vidanapathirana, Abramson, Forbes, & Fairley, 2005).
- Prison-based therapeutic communities are consistently effective in reducing drug use and recidivism, and correctional boot camps are not (Mitchell, Wilson, & MacKenzie, 2006; Wilson, MacKenzie, & Mitchell, 2005).

- Cognitive-behavioral therapy (CBT) is effective in reducing anxiety disorders in children and adolescents (James, Soler, & Weatherall, 2005), but there is insufficient evidence of effects of CBT for child victims of sexual abuse (Macdonald, Higgins, & Ramchandani, 2006).
- Whether provided in clinics or homes, home safety education improves a wide range of safe practices, even in homes with greater risk of injury. There is insufficient evidence on the impact of these programs on injuries to children (Kendrick et al., 2007).
- Welfare-to-work programs have had consistent, small effects on participants' employment and earnings in the United States (Smedslund et al., 2006).

In short, meta-analysis can be used to synthesize information on many topics that are important for social work practice and social policy.

Advantages

Systematic reviews and meta-analysis can overcome important limitations that are inherent in traditional, narrative summaries of research. Systematic methods impose discipline on the review process. Meta-analysis provides an efficient way to summarize results of a large number of studies and can uncover associations not previously identified. There are standards for systematic reviews and meta-analysis, yet existing syntheses vary in quality. When carefully conducted, systematic reviews and meta-analyses offer a transparency not present in traditional, narrative summaries of research findings. Discipline and transparency combine to minimize bias.

What Are the Alternatives?

The present alternatives to systematic reviews are traditional narrative reviews, termed "haphazard" reviews by Petticrew and Roberts (2006).

The alternatives to meta-analysis are narrative summaries and "vote counting." A narrative summary describes the primary studies and comes to conclusions about the weight of the evidence. The process is rarely explicit, so readers may not be able to tell how evidence was weighed and whether conclusions are biased. The synthesis of results across studies is a highly complex task that is not performed reliably with cognitive algebra. Research shows that trivial properties of studies affect readers' assessments of them (Bushman & Wells, 2001). Several studies show that narrative reviews and vote counting can lead to wrong results (Bushman & Wells, 2001; Carlton & Strawderman, 1996).

As the term suggests, vote counting involves merely tallying the numbers of studies that provide positive, null, and negative results. A major limitation of vote counting is its reliance on tests of statistical significance in the primary studies. Significance tests are affected by sample size. In studies with very large samples, *clinically* insignificant differences will be *statistically* significant. Significance tests (p values) do not tell us the strength or magnitude of the effect, so vote counting may tally positive scores that do not really matter (e.g., clinically insignificant effects in large studies).

Conversely, studies based on small samples often lack the statistical power needed to detect meaningful effects. Thus clinically significant effects can be missed when small studies are combined with vote counting. For example, James, Soler, and Weatherall (2005) synthesized results of 12 randomized, controlled trials (RCTs) on the effects of CBT for anxiety disorders among children and adolescents in community outpatient samples. Ten studies had fewer than 100 participants, and six found no significant effects on remission from anxiety. However, when pooled across all 12 studies (with a total of 785 participants), results were clinically and statistically significant, indicating that 56% of youth who received CBT no longer met diagnostic criteria for anxiety disorders, compared with 28.2% of control cases. Applied to the same data, vote counting leads to the conclusion that half of the studies found significant, positive results and half did not.

Another alternative is to ignore statistical significance and count studies that have results in a positive or negative direction; however, this is imprecise and it wastes valuable information. Meta-analysis provides more precise overall summaries of effects and, by combining results from multiple studies, increases the statistical power available to detect significant effects.

Cwikel, Behar, and Rabson-Hare (2000) proposed yet another vote-counting approach that combines information on study quality, defined in terms of ratings of research designs and sample size, with assessments of the strength and consistency of results across all outcome measures. The final vote count was a product of these two assessments. This method confounds study features (design quality and results) that are not necessarily related. Methodologically rigorous studies may find strong treatment effects in one setting (e.g., university clinics) but not others (community agencies). The conflation of design quality and outcomes also means that rigorous studies that show that treatment has little impact (those with high design scores and low outcome scores) will be equated with weak studies that produce positive results (low design scores and high outcome scores). Studies that show positive effects on main outcomes and weaker effects on secondary outcomes are equated with those that produce the opposite pattern. Design-and-outcome scores have no inherent meaning and should be avoided.

Better Parameter Estimates

Due to sampling error, any study can produce an inaccurate estimate of effects in a larger population—that is, even if effects of a treatment are constant in a population, any sample from that population will provide only one estimate of the treatment effect. That estimate can fall anywhere in the sampling distribution around the population parameter and may be affected by Type I or Type II error. Just as well-constructed, multiple-item scales provide more reliable measures of a construct than any single item, the synthesis of results from multiple studies can provide better estimates of population parameters than any single study. To accomplish this, meta-analysis capitalizes on probability theory and includes a number of methods for measuring and partitioning sampling error. We will return to this topic in Chapter 5. For now, it is sufficient to restate the principle that the replication of results (in separate studies) is fundamental to the development of scientific knowledge. Meta-analysis provides quantitative methods for analyzing and synthesizing such replications. An advantage of meta-analysis, therefore, is its ability to provide robust parameter estimates.

Assessment of Outcomes in Multiple Domains

Many studies use multiple outcome measures. When results are mixed, narrative reviews may say just that. However, narrative reviews appear vulnerable to confirmation bias and seem to be biased toward positive effects (Littell, in press). Meta-analysis can produce more precise information about mixed results by quantitatively summarizing effects in each of several outcome domains. A recent meta-analysis shows that in-home or clinic-based home safety education actually improves a wide range of safety practices in the home environment (e.g., safe water temperature, storage of dangerous chemicals, use of smoke detectors); however, there is no evidence that education alone reduces the risk of injury to children (Kendrick et al., 2007).

Moderator Analysis

Narrative reviews cannot systematically account for moderators—that is, participant, treatment, or study design characteristics that influence the variables under study. Meta-analysis uses moderator analysis to assess such influences on variations in effect size. If moderator analyses indicate that certain characteristics do not have an influence on the overall effect, then these findings suggest that results are robust and may be transferable to other settings. If the studies are inconsistent between settings, the sources of variation can be examined (Glasziou et al., 2001). Recall that Wilson, Lipsey, and Soydan (2003) found mainstream programs for juveniles to be just as effective for minority and majority youth. In the home safety education meta-analysis described above, investigators found that these interventions were no less effective for families whose children were at greater risk of injury (Kendrick et al., 2007).

Social workers know that many interventions have differential effects; one size rarely fits all. Moderator analysis can specify the characteristics of participants who are most and least likely to benefit from an intervention. This can enhance efforts to target interventions to those most likely to benefit. Moderator analysis can also identify dose effects and approaches to treatment that are most likely to succeed. We will return to this topic in Chapter 6.

Minimizing Error and Bias

Meta-analysis can minimize sampling error and bias in attempts to synthesize the growing body of empirical research relevant to social work. Thus, it has an important role in the development of knowledge for human services. Even so, many lists of "evidence-based" practices are not based on meta-analyses. The traditional, narrative research reviews that often are used to identify "effective" or model programs are vulnerable to many sources and types of bias (Littell, in press), some of which are mentioned above. A more systematic approach is needed to provide unbiased assessments of evidence (Littell, 2005).

Since meta-analysis is time consuming and requires training and discipline, it is not likely to be conducted by practitioners or policy makers. However, doctoral students and social work scholars can use meta-analysis to make important contributions to the knowledge base for all of the helping professions. This can be a tremendous contribution to consumers, practitioners, and policy makers who want to use accurate assessments of current knowledge to inform their choices.

Like any tool, meta-analysis can be (and has been) badly misused. Thus, it is very important to consider its limitations.

Criticisms of Meta-Analysis

The most common criticisms of meta-analysis are not related to meta-analysis per se but to illogical applications and misuse of meta-analytic techniques. There are, however, some legitimate concerns about the use of meta-analytic techniques. Here we discuss both issues.

First, it is important to plainly state an uncomfortable truth: many published meta-analyses in social work, psychology, and education (and a few in medicine) are based on outdated techniques and are vulnerable to known sources of bias (discussed below). Thus, while meta-analysis has the potential to provide useful information for social work practice and policy, it can also produce information that is invalid and misleading. While extreme, one example is that meta-analyses funded by pharmaceutical companies have consistently produced results more favorable to their own products than meta-analyses conducted by independent investigators (Jørgensen, Hilden, & Gøtzsche, 2006). Like any form of research, systematic reviews and meta-analysis are not immune to bias.

Second, while meta-analysis requires considerable effort and expertise, the techniques should not overshadow substantive issues. A highly structured enterprise, meta-analysis provides useful discipline, but in the hands of analysts who are not sensitive to important substantive issues (e.g., theoretical constructs, contextual effects) it can become a meaningless, merely statistical exercise.

Inadequate Conceptualization of the Problem

Conceptual problems often arise with regard to the lumping and splitting decisions that go into meta-analysis. For instance, what kinds of treatment can be combined legitimately? Absent a strong conceptual rationale, decisions to pool results across different types of treatments, samples, or outcomes may produce results that are difficult to interpret. This is the classic criticism of meta-analysis—it combines apples and oranges. Prominent meta-analysts (Glass, Cooper, and others) have often noted that such combinations are appropriate when one is interested in fruit salad; however, they are not appropriate when one is interested in apples or wants to distinguish apples from oranges. In other words, a meta-analysis must have clear objectives and a strong conceptual framework to guide the work so that it will produce meaningful results. We consider these issues further in Chapter 2.

Inadequate Assessment of Study Quality

A meta-analysis of weak studies (i.e., studies that provide very limited support for inferences due to unreliable measures, design flaws, or implementation problems) will produce unreliable results. This problem is often termed "garbage in, garbage out."

To combat this, meta-analysts must establish—at the outset—thoughtful criteria for the kinds of research designs and interventions (if applicable) to be included in the analysis. What kinds of study designs are defensible given the questions and subject matter of interest? What kinds of interventions represent the independent variables of interest? We return to these topics in Chapter 2.

Even with clear inclusion criteria, we may encounter surprises once we have studied the included studies carefully. For example, in a meta-analysis that was limited to RCTs, Littell, Popa, and Forsythe (2005) found that some of the trials were not implemented well, which reduced confidence in the results. The solution is to assess the quality of included studies carefully, a topic that we address in Chapter 3.

Low External Validity

As with any form of research, results of meta-analyses can be generalized only to settings, populations, interventions, and contexts similar to those under investigation (Shadish, 1995; Shadish, Cook, & Campbell, 2002). University-based treatments are often characterized by higher methodological rigor (experimental designs), homogeneous samples, a single problem focus, intensive training of therapists, and manualized treatment. Therefore, results from these types of settings cannot be generalized to typical social work practice settings, which are characterized by diverse clients with a multitude of problems, a lack of training and supervision of therapists, and large caseloads and high paperwork requirements of staff. In some ways, efficacy studies will not be as important for social work as studies of effectiveness (impacts of treatments under less than ideal conditions). This suggests a need for more studies of effectiveness and greater emphasis on these types of studies in meta-analyses.

Reliance on Effect Sizes

To combine studies quantitatively, it is necessary to obtain measures that are comparable across studies. Attempts to obtain such comparable measures have yielded a group of indices labeled effect sizes (ESs). These tell us the strength or magnitude of the relationships between variables. In meta-analysis, ESs are calculated for each study, weighted by sample size, and then averaged to produce an overall effect. There are many ways to calculate ES, and it is critical that only ESs of the same type be combined (Lipsey & Wilson, 2001). These different methods are presented in Chapter 4.

Meta-analysis has been criticized for its reliance on ES. Although ES provides a crucial index of the average effect within and across studies, it is not easily understood by many people. This limitation can be overcome by translating ES into metrics that have meaning for clinicians and policy makers. Scher and colleagues (2006) provide an example of how this can be done by reporting results in ES metrics and also in raw percentages (the latter are shown in Figure 1.1).

Newer Techniques Have Not Yet Been Validated

Some newer meta-analytic techniques have not yet been validated. For example, techniques used to detect and correct for publication bias are still under debate (Rothstein, Sutton, & Bornstein, 2005). We will discuss this more fully in Chapter 6.

Short Shelf Life

Meta-analyses need to be updated to reflect current knowledge in the field. Several studies are investigating how often meta-analyses need to be updated and how to tell whether new studies could alter previous conclusions (David Moher, personal communication, July 2007; Alex Sutton, personal communication, July 2007).

Ignoring Valuable Qualitative Information

Although meta-analysis cannot be used to synthesize qualitative (non-numeric) data, qualitative information can inform meta-analyses by suggesting issues and contrasts that may matter, providing contextual information, and illuminating intervention processes. For example, qualitative data on current policy contexts may be helpful in understanding cross-national differences in responses to certain interventions.

Inadequate Sampling and Data Collection Methods

We have saved for last our biggest concerns about published meta-analyses. These are not criticisms of meta-analysis per se; rather they reflect insufficient attention to potential sources of error and bias in sampling and evaluating studies for meta-analysis. The two problems are reliance on published studies (inadequate sampling) and lack of attention to the reliability and validity of data extraction from studies.

Many meta-analyses are based solely on published studies. Although a few studies find no systematic differences between published and unpublished studies (e.g., De Smidt & Gorey, 1997), a much larger and very compelling literature finds considerable publication and dissemination biases in the behavioral, social, and health sciences.

Outcome Reporting Bias

In studies with mixed results, statistically significant results are more likely to be reported than null findings (Chan et al., 2004; Williamson & Gamble, 2005; Williamson et al., 2006). This is known as *outcome reporting bias*. Chan and colleagues (2004) have shown that even when mixed results are reported, statistically significant results tend to be presented in greater detail than null findings. This means that it is easier for meta-analysts to calculate ESs for results that run counter to the null hypothesis. Unless this tendency is checked, it will produce upwardly biased ESs.

Publication bias refers to the concern that published studies do not represent all the high-quality studies in a field of inquiry. There is now convincing evidence that studies with positive, statistically significant results are more likely to be submitted for publication and more likely to appear in print than studies with negative or null results (Begg, 1994; Dickersin, 2005; Scherer, Langenberg, & von Elm, 2007; Torgerson, 2006). The sources of this bias are complex and involve authors' decisions as well as those of journal editors. Selective publication and citation of reports with positive findings makes those results more visible and available than others (Dickersin, 2005).

Dissemination Bias

Other sources of bias in dissemination are related to issues of language, availability, familiarity, and cost of research reports (Rothstein, Sutton, & Bornstein, 2005). Specifically, compared to studies with null results, those with statistically significant results are published more quickly (Hopewell, Clarke, Stewart, & Tierney, 2001), are cited and reprinted more often (Egger & Smith, 1998), and may be more likely to be published in English than other languages (Egger et al., 1997c). Thus, studies with statistically significant results are easier to locate and more readily available in English than equally rigorous studies with different results. This bias is likely to appear in meta-analyses that are limited to published studies (Lipsey & Wilson, 1993), and it can lead to wrong conclusions (Rothstein, Sutton, & Bornstein, 2005).

Study Eligibility Decisions

A research synthesis is vulnerable to bias when reviewers sample studies selectively. Therefore, it is important to set clear inclusion criteria at the outset and demonstrate that these criteria have been consistently followed.

Assessing Study Quality

As journals impose tighter page limits on research articles and as "Methods" sections shrink, it becomes more difficult to determine exactly what was done in published studies. Some authors have suggested that one reader could reliably assess studies if he or she did this twice over time and then compared results. However, we know of no data on whether one person's reading (or misreading) of a study report remains consistent over time. It is clear, however, that different assessors arrive at different understandings of the methods used in primary studies. Another problem is that different study quality scales produce different results (see Chapter 4).

Data Extraction

Many reviewers seem overconfident in their ability to reliably extract and evaluate information from completed studies. Unless key decisions about study eligibility, study quality, and outcomes are extracted by independent raters—and unless results of interrater agreement are reported—readers cannot know whether these procedures were reliable. A recent study found data extraction errors in 10 (37%) of 27 meta-analyses (Gøtzsche, Hrógjartsson, Marić, & Tendal, 2007). Obviously, meta-analysis cannot produce precise estimates without avoiding data entry and calculation errors.

For all the reasons noted in the preceding paragraphs, meta-analyses should be embedded in systematic reviews, which aim to minimize sources of error and bias at each step in the review process.

Steps in a Systematic Review and Meta-Analysis

The systematic review process includes several phases that are parallel to those of primary research (see Table 1.2). These include problem formulation, sampling, data collection, data analysis, interpretation, and

Table 1.2. Steps in the Systematic Review Process Are Parallel to Steps in Survey Research

Step	Systematic Review	Survey Research
Topic formulation	Central questions, hypotheses, objectives	Central questions, hypotheses, objectives
Overall study design	Protocol development	Protocol development
	Specify problems/conditions, populations, settings, interventions, and outcomes of interest	Specify key constructs, information needs
	Specify study inclusion and exclusion criteria	Specify sample characteristics
Sampling	Develop a sampling plan	Develop a sampling plan
	Sampling unit is the study	Sampling unit may be the individual, household, or group
	Consider universe of all potentially relevant studies	Identify sampling frame (all relevant sampling units)
	Obtain studies	Sample units
Data collection	Data are derived (extracted) from studies onto standardized forms	Data are collected from individuals via self-administered surveys or interviews
Data analysis	Descriptive data (examine study qualities, samples, and intervention characteristics; compute effect sizes)	Descriptive data (examine qualitative and categorical data, frequencies and distributions on continuous variables)
	Pool effect sizes and assess heterogeneity (meta-analysis)	Measures of central tendency and variability
	Cumulative meta-analysis, subgroup and moderator analysis, sensitivity analysis, analysis of publication and small-sample bias	Bivariate and exploratory analyses
	Meta-regression	Multivariate analyses

(continued)

Table 1.2. (*continued*)

Step	Systematic Review	Survey Research
Reporting	Description of results in narrative, tables, and graphs	Description of results in narrative, tables, and graphs
	Interpretation and discussion	Interpretation and discussion
	Implications for policy, practice, and further research	Implications for policy, practice, and further research

presentation of results (Cooper, 1998). Specifically, systematic reviews involve the following steps:

- Develop a set of clearly formulated objectives and specific, answerable research questions or hypotheses. This is best done in consultation with people who are likely to use results of the review (practitioners, policy makers, and consumers).
- Form a review team that includes people with the diverse skills necessary (including substantive, methodological, and technical expertise).
- Create explicit inclusion and exclusion criteria that specify the problems, conditions, populations, interventions, settings, comparisons, outcomes, and study designs that will and will not be included in the review.
- Develop a written protocol that details in advance the procedures and methods to be used.
- In collaboration with information specialists, identify and implement a comprehensive and reproducible strategy to identify all relevant studies. This includes strategies to find unpublished studies.
- Screen titles and abstracts to identify potentially relevant studies.
- Retrieve published and unpublished reports on potentially relevant studies.
- Determine whether each study meets the review's eligibility criteria. Two reviewers judge each study, resolve disagreements (sometimes with a third reviewer), and document their decisions.

- Reliably extract data from eligible studies onto standardized forms. Assess interrater reliability, resolve disagreements, and document decisions.
- Systematically and critically appraise the qualities of included studies. As before, this should be done by two raters who resolve disagreements and document decisions.
- Describe key features of included studies (through narrative, tables, and/or graphs).
- Present study results in ES metrics, with 95% confidence intervals.

If a systematic review lends itself to *combining* quantitative results of two or more primary studies, then it can (and often should) include meta-analysis to perform one or more of the tasks below:

- estimate overall (mean) effects,
- assess variations (heterogeneity) in effects across studies,
- assess trends in effects over time,
- assess effects for prespecified subgroups of the population of interest,
- explore the potential impact of moderators (study, sample, or treatment characteristics) on ESs,
- assess impacts of decisions made during the review process, and
- assess the potential impact on results of publication bias and small-sample bias.

In sum, there are many steps in the systematic review process and in meta-analysis. These steps are detailed throughout the remainder of this book.

Quality Standards

The QUOROM statement was developed to enhance the **Qu**ality **o**f **R**eporting **o**n **M**eta-analyses of RCTs (Moher et al., 1999). The QUOROM statement is a living document based on empirical evidence and expert consensus. Given the above-mentioned concerns about the conduct of meta-analysis outside of systematic reviews, the QUOROM group is updating its standards and changing its name to PRISMA (**P**rimary **R**eporting **I**tems for **S**ystematic **R**eviews and **M**eta-**A**nalysis).

A recent study indicates that use of protocols and study quality assessments has increased, but there have been few improvements in the quality of reporting on systematic reviews indexed in MEDLINE (Moher et al., 2007). Since the quality of published meta-analyses and systematic reviews is uneven, readers should not accept these studies uncritically. Standards for assessing the methodological quality of systematic reviews have been developed, based on empirical evidence and expert consensus (Shea et al., 2007). The recent AMSTAR (**A**ssessment of **M**ultiple **S**ystematic **R**eviews) statement can be found in Appendix A.

Key Organizations

A number of governmental and nonprofit organizations sponsor or produce systematic reviews and meta-analyses of empirical research. Of particular relevance for social work are two international, interdisciplinary collaborations of scholars, policy makers, practitioners, and consumers. The Cochrane Collaboration synthesizes results of studies on effects of interventions in health care (www.cochrane.org), and the Campbell Collaboration synthesizes results of research on interventions in the fields of social care (education, social welfare, and crime and justice; www.campbellcollaboration.org). Both groups produce systematic reviews and meta-analyses to inform decisions about health and social programs and policies. Both are devoted to minimizing error and bias in research synthesis. Building on advances in the science of research synthesis, these groups have produced background papers and evidence-based guidelines for reviewers (e.g., Becker, Hedges, & Pigott, 2004; Higgins & Green, 2006; Rothstein, Turner, & Lavenberg, 2004; Shadish & Myers, 2004), along with studies of methodological qualities of systematic reviews (e.g., Hopewell, Clarke, Lefebvre, & Scherer, 2006; Hopewell, McDonald, Clarke, & Egger, 2006). Because their interests overlap, the two collaborations have a number of joint groups devoted to the development of review methods and production of systematic reviews.

Contrary to common misconceptions, Cochrane and Campbell reviews are not limited to RCTs. However, for reasons we take up in Chapter 2, both groups emphasize RCTs in systematic reviews of intervention effects (Higgins & Green, 2006; Shadish & Myers, 2004). But Cochrane and Campbell reviews are not limited to studies of intervention effects. For example, the Cochrane Collaboration has begun to conduct reviews on the accuracy of diagnostic tests and the prognostic accuracy of tests. While RCTs are appropriate for studies of intervention effects, they are obviously not appropriate for all of the research questions that can be addressed with systematic reviews and meta-analysis.

Prominent social work scholars have been involved in these collaborations for many years. Reviewers can submit titles and protocols for systematic reviews to either collaboration. Both collaborations provide technical and editorial assistance, use rigorous peer-review processes, and produce systematic reviews and meta-analyses in a variety of formats.

The Science of Research Synthesis

The science of research synthesis exists to enhance the reliability and validity of research reviews and meta-analyses. This science is rapidly advancing through studies of the relative strengths and weaknesses of different approaches to locating, analyzing, and synthesizing results of empirical research. Methodological studies in this area are producing a body of knowledge that can be used to minimize error and bias in research synthesis and enhance the validity of inferences drawn from a body of research using meta-analysis and related techniques. Many of these studies can be found in the Cochrane Database of Systematic Reviews (under the topic heading "methodology review") and in journals such as the *British Medical Journal*, *Statistics in Medicine*, and *Psychological Methods*. In 2005, the Society for Research Synthesis Methodology

(SRSM) emerged to further the development of all aspects of the systematic review process, including meta-analysis (www.srsm.org).

Purpose and Organization of the Book

This book aims to familiarize graduate students and social work scholars with current methods and standards for research synthesis. It will show you how to read and critically appraise systematic reviews and meta-analyses, and help you begin to design and conduct credible and useful reviews and syntheses of your own. We emphasize the concepts essential to understanding, critiquing, and conducting research synthesis—not the statistical underpinnings. We show you the logic of systematic reviews and meta-analysis and how to consider different approaches. We discuss decisions encountered in the review process and the rationale for certain choices, pointing to empirical evidence of the consequences of those choices when that evidence is available. Examples are drawn from the field of social work, and the methods and standards we describe are germane to the state of social work research.

The book will prepare you to engage in more technical aspects of systematic reviews and meta-analysis, should you choose to do so. Statistics for meta-analysis are covered elsewhere (Lipsey & Wilson, 2001, is an excellent resource), and many formulas are built into available software programs. References to these works, along with more advanced texts and many other useful resources for further information about systematic review methods and meta-analysis, are provided throughout the book.

The book is organized according to the steps involved in conducting a meta-analysis within a systematic review. For convenience, we will use the term "review" to connote a systematic review that contains meta-analysis. Chapter 2 considers issues in formulating a topic and developing a protocol (plan) for the review. Chapter 3 discusses how to locate relevant studies and determine whether they are eligible for further review and meta-analysis. Chapter 4 demonstrates how to extract data from included studies and assess their methodological quality. Chapter 5 covers different measures of ES and methods used to pool (combine) ESs across studies. Chapter 6 describes techniques for assessing bias and possible sources of variations in effects, including tests for publication and small-sample bias, cumulative meta-analysis, subgroup and moderator analysis, meta-regression, and sensitivity analysis. Chapter 6 also includes a brief discussion of statistical power in meta-analysis. Chapter 7 considers essential issues for interpreting and summarizing systematic reviews and meta-analyses, along with the present and future of research synthesis and its implications for social work. Appendices describe available software for meta-analysis and guidelines for conducting and reporting meta-analyses in systematic reviews.

Main Points: Chapter 1

- Systematic reviews and meta-analyses can contribute to the evidence base for social work practice and policy by providing thorough and unbiased summaries of empirical research.
- A systematic review aims to comprehensively locate and synthesize the research literature that bears on a particular question.
  - If results lend themselves to the synthesis of findings from two or more primary studies, then a systematic review can include meta-analysis.
- Meta-analysis is the quantitative synthesis of data from multiple studies.
- Systematic reviews and meta-analyses offer many advantages over traditional narrative reviews, including:
  - greater transparency,
  - detection and reduction of bias,
  - better estimates of population parameters,
  - ability to assess outcomes in multiple domains, and
  - systematic accounts for moderators (participant, treatment, or study design characteristics) that influence outcomes.

- Systematic reviews and meta-analyses have disadvantages as well:
  - They cannot make up for poor quality in the original studies.
  - Combining results across different types of studies, treatments, samples, settings, and/or outcomes is not always appropriate.
  - Meta-analysis relies on effect sizes, which are not easily understood by many people.
  - Some newer meta-analytic techniques have yet to be validated.
  - Reviews need to be updated to reflect current knowledge in the field.
  - Many reviews ignore information offered by qualitative studies.
- Many of the disadvantages can be eliminated or minimized through procedures recommended in this book.
- At present, the quality of systematic reviews and meta-analyses is uneven. Some are based on outdated techniques and are subject to bias.
- Quality standards are available for systematic reviews and meta-analyses.
- A number of government and nonprofit organizations sponsor or produce systematic reviews and meta-analyses, including the Cochrane Collaboration and the Campbell Collaboration.

For Further Reading

Higgins, J. P. T., & Green, S. (Eds.) (2006). *Cochrane handbook for systematic reviews of interventions.* Chichester, UK: John Wiley & Sons.

Lipsey, M. W., & Wilson, D. B. (2001). *Practical meta-analysis.* Thousand Oaks, CA: SAGE Publications.

Petticrew, M., & Roberts, H. (2006). *Systematic reviews in the social sciences: A practical guide.* Oxford, UK: Blackwell Publishing.

2

Formulating a Topic and Developing a Protocol

Good planning is essential to the success of any research project. Important tasks and issues that arise in planning a systematic review and meta-analysis are considered in this chapter. We begin with discussion of the composition of the review team and ways to involve "end users" and advisory boards in the planning process. Next we consider how to develop and refine a topic, articulate central questions or hypotheses, and affix the scope of a review. We explain the use of specific inclusion and exclusion criteria to clarify central concepts and set the boundaries of a review. Finally, we discuss the development of a formal title and protocol for the review.

There is some flexibility in the order in which these steps are taken. For example, the review team could be formed at the beginning, middle, or end of the planning process.

The Review Team

A systematic review and meta-analysis requires diverse skills and perspectives, including knowledge of substantive issues, information science, and methods of research synthesis. In-depth knowledge of the subject matter is essential in order to develop a strong conceptual framework that can guide a rigorous and relevant review. Knowledge of the field of inquiry is required to articulate meaningful inclusion and exclusion criteria, to inform decisions that are made throughout the review and meta-analysis, and to interpret results.

Information science is developing at an unprecedented rate. As we will suggest in the next chapter, reviewers should not underestimate the importance of technical know-how in identifying and accessing relevant databases, crafting sensitive and efficient search strategies, dealing with language biases, and finding the "gray" and "fugitive" (unpublished or hard-to-find) literature. A review team must enlist the help of information scientists if it is to use this technical knowledge to best advantage.

The science of research synthesis (systematic review and meta-analytic methods) is also advancing at a very rapid rate. Thus, it is important that someone on the team be familiar with current methodological developments (or have the capacity and willingness to learn about them).

Few individuals possess all of the qualities mentioned above. Further, the systematic review process and meta-analysis are labor intensive, requiring patience and exacting attention to detail. Teamwork is essential. The team must develop procedures to ensure interrater agreement to minimize error and bias in study screening and coding decisions. For all of these reasons, the Cochrane and Campbell Collaborations do not accept single-authored reviews. Reviewers can contact the collaborations to find potential collaborators who have expertise in needed areas.

Involving Users

Most systematic reviews are meant to be useful for practice and policy. Nowhere is this more important than in social work and social welfare, where applications of evidence matter. Policy makers, practitioners, and consumers will interpret results of systematic reviews and meta-analyses—whether reviewers have planned for this or not. When the relevance for practice or policy is unclear, or when results are hard to comprehend, users are likely to decide that a review is not useful. As with primary research, the relevance and utilization of systematic reviews can be enhanced by involving potential users in shaping questions and objectives at the beginning, and interpreting results at the end, of a review.

There are several ways to involve users in planning and developing a systematic review. Reviewers can meet with practitioners and policy makers to discuss their work. Some reviewers include a practitioner, policy maker, or consumer as a member of the review team. Health-care consumers are often consulted in the development and interpretation of Cochrane reviews. Another alternative is to create an advisory board comprising experts in relevant areas of practice and policy who can be called upon to provide feedback throughout the review process. Of course, these approaches can be combined.

The potential value of users' input on the central questions, objectives, and inclusion and exclusion criteria for a review cannot be overstated. This input can make the difference between a review that is an interesting exercise and one that has value for practice.

Topic and Scope

As in any research, the first step in a research synthesis is to identify the central questions (or hypotheses) that will guide the review. At the outset it is also important to clarify the purposes of a review, as well as its focus, scope, and central assumptions. A clear, logical framework will serve as a guide for the remaining stages of the review.

Good questions and hypotheses come from many sources: practice experience, results of prior research, and critical appraisal of the literature are but a few origins. There is no shortage of important topics for empirical inquiry in social work and the social and behavioral sciences.

What makes a good research question? Cummings, Browner, and Hulley (1988) proposed the FINER criteria: research questions should be feasible (specific and answerable), interesting, novel, ethical, and relevant. "Does [an intervention] work?" is not a specific or answerable question because it implies a yes-or-no answer, and intervention effects are not that simple. First, the most effective interventions don't work for everyone, and the least effective treatments might work in some instances. Second, effectiveness is a relative notion: there is always an implicit or explicit comparison. The question "Does it work?" does not include the important modifier "Compared to what?" Therefore, it is important to specify the populations, conditions, contrasts, and outcomes of interest. A better formula for questions about intervention effects is as follows: "Is [intervention X1] more effective than [intervention X2] in addressing [Y outcomes] in [Z population or context]?"

When selecting a topic, consider what purposes could be served by synthesizing knowledge in this area. How might a synthesis of information on this topic be used, and by whom (policy makers, practitioners, or consumers)? Again, discussing the topic with potential users of the review will help investigators frame the topic in relevant ways and decide how broad or narrow the topic should be and what components (populations, conditions, treatments, settings, contrasts, outcomes) should be included and excluded.

The scope of a systematic review may be broad or narrow depending on its purposes and how the central problem is conceptualized. For example, one review might assess effects of after-school programs on a wide range of outcomes related to child well-being (self-efficacy, peer relations, academic achievement, illicit substance use). Another might focus on effects of these programs for low-income children. A third could focus on a restricted range or a single outcome, such as academic achievement. These topics reflect different research questions. Each approach is useful for different purposes. Since reviews that are broad in scope are more expensive than more narrowly focused reviews, the choice also depends on available resources.

Equally important is the "lumping and splitting" problem mentioned earlier—that is, what kinds of interventions, samples, and target outcomes may be combined legitimately, and which should be kept separate? There is no single, correct set of answers to this question. Just as no people are identical (even identical twins differ), no two studies are exactly alike; thus, there will *always* be some substantive (or clinical) heterogeneity in a meta-analysis. Logical and relevant combinations and distinctions are constructed in the context of a well-thought-out review; they depend on the central question and how key constructs are conceptualized. The "apples and oranges" problem can be resolved at the outset by carefully considering what "fruits" are of interest and how they relate to each other. Methods for assessing heterogeneity will be discussed in Chapters 5 and 6.

Conceptualization of the problem draws on our understanding of the issues at stake, key constructs, and important causes and consequences. Social and behavioral theories provide many useful ideas that can guide conceptualization of key constructs and relationships among them. Logic models provide a useful way to articulate and examine these understandings and assumptions. Logic models use a diagram format to illustrate hypothesized relationships between pretreatment conditions, interventions, and short-term and long-term outcomes. Providing "an easy-to-understand visual representation of the overall topic area" (p. 433), logic models are useful for identifying outcomes that need to be considered, including benefits and harms; defining which linkage(s) will be the centerpiece of the review; and assessing whether important outcomes, causes, or interventions have been overlooked (Zaza, Briss, & Harris, 2005).

Zief, Lauver, and Maynard (2006) developed a logic model (shown in Figure 2.1) to guide their systematic review and meta-analysis of effects of after-school programs. They drew on conceptual models developed in previous studies of the processes and outcomes of after-school programs (Dynarski, James-Burdumy, Mansfield, Mayer, Moore, Mullens, & Silva, 2001; Lauver, 2002; cited in Zief et al., 2006). Accompanied by narrative discussion of the meanings of key concepts (boxes) and assumptions about causal relationships (arrows), a logic model can guide further conceptualization of the review and meta-analysis processes. It is a useful tool for framing study inclusion and exclusion criteria (e.g., explaining why some outcomes are included and others are not) and will aid in the design of a strategy for synthesizing data across studies.

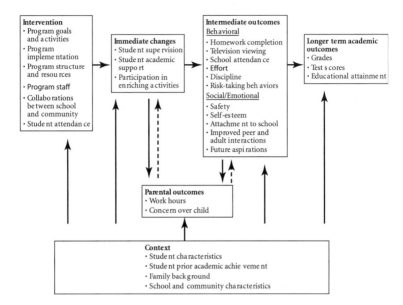

Figure 2.1. Logic model for understanding the theory of change for low-income elementary youth in an afterschool program. *Source*: Zief, Lauver, & Maynard, 2006.

When logic models are complex, reviewers (perhaps in consultation with users) may decide to limit the review to one specific pathway in the model. Members of the CDC Task Force on Community Preventive Services have used logic models to identify important topics for systematic reviews. These have been distilled into specific analytic frameworks for reviews of evidence on early childhood development programs for low-income children (Anderson et al., 2003c), tenant-based rental assistance programs (Anderson et al., 2003a), and efforts to create culturally competent health-care systems (Anderson et al., 2003b).

At this point in the formulation of a topic, it may be useful to assess our motivations, assumptions, and biases. What are our a priori assumptions about what the results will show? What if we are completely wrong? Can we accept the full range of possible results? (If the answer to the last question is no, reviewers might want to consider a different topic.)

Study Eligibility Criteria

The next step is to formulate specific eligibility criteria to determine what kinds of studies should be included or excluded in the review. Again, it is important to develop clear criteria at the outset to guide the study selection process and other critical decisions that will be made in the review and meta-analysis. Study eligibility criteria specify the study designs, populations, interventions, comparisons, and outcome measures to be included and excluded. These criteria should be derived from the overall conceptual model described above. Ideally, this will be done in consultation with users.

The a priori specification of selection criteria limits reviewers' freedom to select studies on the basis of their results or on some other basis, protecting the review from unexamined selection bias. If specific selection criteria are not set up at the beginning, inclusion decisions may be based on ideological views, personal preferences, convenience, or other factors. In any case, the reader will be left to guess how and why some studies were included and others were not. Clear eligibility criteria allow savvy readers to determine whether relevant studies were omitted and/or irrelevant studies included. Explicit inclusion and exclusion criteria also provide clear boundaries so that the review can be replicated or extended by others.

To delineate the domains of inclusion criteria, we begin with the PICO framework widely used for this purpose in the Cochrane Collaboration. PICO stands for **p**opulations, **i**nterventions, **c**omparisons, and **o**utcomes—four topics that should be addressed in detail in developing study eligibility criteria. This framework has been adapted by the Campbell Collaboration and others.

To create eligibility criteria, we specify the characteristics we are looking for in study populations, interventions, comparisons, and outcomes. Having stated the criteria and reasons for inclusion, we may want to add exclusion criteria to identify important characteristics that would lead us to rule out a study. Examples are provided in the sections that follow.

Participants

In the primary studies included in a review, participants are usually individuals. However, for some purposes participants could be defined as households or families, organizations, communities, or other social groups. Participants are often the targets of intervention (clients), as well as the sources and/or subjects of data collection on outcomes. Participant inclusion criteria indicate who is involved in the primary studies of interest and why these people (or groups) were chosen.

For systematic reviews on interventions that target individuals, it is often important to consider participants' developmental status or life stage. For example, Scher and colleagues (2006) examined pregnancy prevention programs that targeted middle school and high school youth, but they performed separate analyses for these groups. Depending on the topic, it may be important to specify other demographic characteristics, such as gender, race, socioeconomic status, family composition, location (rural, urban), and so forth.

Exclusion criteria often identify important conditions that would preclude participants from involvement in the treatment of interest (e.g., cognitive impairment or psychosis). For example, a review of Multisystemic Therapy (MST) for youth with social, emotional, and behavioral problems explicitly excluded studies in which the primary presenting problem was a medical condition, such as diabetes (Littell, Popa, & Forsythe, 2005).

Here the lumping and splitting problem (that is, which participant groups should be included, combined, kept separate, excluded, etc.) can be considered in terms of how different types of participants are treated in the interventions of interest. Should we include families of abused and neglected children in the same review? Since child abuse and neglect often co-occur, many interventions target both problems; however, there are specialized programs that deal only with neglect, physical abuse, or sexual abuse. The decision to lump these groups together or keep them separate depends on the intervention of interest. What are its goals? What groups are the targets of this intervention?

Taking this example further, should we include child welfare, mental health, and juvenile justice populations in a single review? While there is considerable overlap between these groups, the three service sectors are quite separate in some jurisdictions. However, if an intervention is purported to be effective with youth across a wide range of social, emotional, and behavioral problems—and across different service sectors—then it is reasonable to use meta-analysis to test that claim. Any claim about the generalizability of treatment effects is fair game for meta-analysis. When many studies are available, subgroup and moderator analysis can be used to explore differential effects in different groups (see Chapter 6), but there are simply not enough studies to do this in many areas.

Interventions

Inclusion criteria should specify the intervention(s) of interest and provide a brief summary of the nature of the intervention, including its goals; theoretical foundations; key techniques or activities; staff qualifications; and typical frequency, intensity, and duration. It is sometimes necessary to specify use of particular treatment manuals, staff training experiences, or certification or licensing requirements. For example, the MST review included studies of licensed MST programs (which implied an array of requirements for training and supervision) and excluded programs that used the term "MST" but were not licensed. Exclusion criteria are used to bound the interventions of interest and identify outliers. For example, a meta-analysis of a brief treatment might exclude interventions that last longer than 8 (or 12) weeks.

To avoid the "apples and oranges" problem with respect to interventions, it is critical that treatments be grouped in ways that are meaningful *for purposes of the review*. A review aimed at assessing effects of crisis intervention programs might include a diverse set of interventions that address different problems (e.g., suicidal ideation, trauma exposure) but rely explicitly on crisis intervention theory. Presumably, the central question would be whether interventions based on crisis intervention theory are more effective than those that are not. Moderator analysis could be used to see whether different treatments had different effects, but it is appropriate to include a heterogeneous set of treatments if the purpose is to test applications of a theory or principle that cuts across different interventions or fields of practice. The analyst should specify what these interventions have in common, and why they are expected to work in similar ways. If the analyst cannot explain these similarities (e.g., in a logic model), the programs may be too diverse for meaningful synthesis. In short, whether a set of interventions is sufficiently homogeneous depends on the central questions, purposes, and logic model of the review. Units that are sufficiently homogeneous in one review will be too diverse to address the central questions of another, and insufficiently diverse to answer central questions in a third review.

Comparisons

We should specify the conditions that will be compared to treatments of interest and the nature of these comparisons. Will the review include studies that use no-treatment control groups, attention/placebo controls, wait-listed groups, comparison groups that receive treatment as usual (TAU, or usual services), and/or comparisons that receive alternative treatment? Studies with wait-listed controls will not provide long-term comparisons. TAU and alternative treatment conditions should be well defined; since these can vary, it may be necessary to specify *which* "usual services" or alternative treatments will and will not be compared to the treatments of interest.

Contrasts between one intervention and another (TAU or an alternative) provide information about *relative* effects of treatment. Contrasts with no-treatment control groups provide evidence of *absolute* effects (including placebo effects). Reviewers must decide which contrasts they wish to make. If both are of interest, each comparison condition should be kept separate in the analysis.

Outcomes

It is important to distinguish primary and secondary outcomes. Primary outcomes reflect the central goals and expected results of an intervention. Secondary outcomes include additional possible benefits and potential harms. Whether primary or secondary, we should identify outcomes that are important for theoretical or practical reasons. Trivial outcomes and those that are not conceptually linked to the treatment of interest should be avoided. The *Cochrane Handbook* advises reviewers to include "all reported outcomes that are likely to be meaningful to people making a decision about the . . . problem the review addresses" (Higgins & Green, 2006).

Logic models are useful for identifying primary and secondary outcomes because they show hypothesized causal links between treatment and outcomes. For example, the logic model developed by Zief and colleagues in their meta-analysis of effects of after-school programs (see Fig. 2.1) shows that enhancing long-term academic outcomes is the ultimate goal of such programs (Zief, Lauver, & Maynard, 2006). Outcomes that don't fit into a logic model should not be included in the meta-analysis.

Since the outcomes of social and health services are complex, it is often insufficient to rely on a single outcome measure. Thus, most program evaluations obtain data on multiple outcomes. This is appropriate when it reflects the multiple goals of intervention, but it is problematic when part of a "fishing expedition" to find significant results. Thus, it may be useful to specify which outcomes will be excluded from the analysis. To be of maximum value to practitioners, policy makers, and funders, meta-analysts often emphasize behavioral outcomes rather than client satisfaction or changes in knowledge or attitudes.

It is important to consider the types of outcome measures to be included and excluded in view of their *reliability* and *validity*. Some meta-analysts limit self-reports to those that are obtained on standardized instruments. However, an instrument that has been standardized on general populations may not be appropriate for a particular subgroup. Some studies obtain information from collateral contacts and triangulate information from different data sources to establish their reliability or validity. Unfortunately, there is very little attention paid to the validity of outcome measures in many studies, and analysts may be left with measures of unknown validity. Thus, reviewers should make decisions in advance about what kinds of measures they will and will not accept. This sets a standard for the review. For example, self-reported use of illicit substances is notoriously underestimated; therefore, in a review in which substance use outcomes are critical, reviewers might rely on drug tests and accept self-reports only if they have been validated by biological measures.

The *timing* of outcome measures should also be considered. Immediate post-treatment measures of outcome do not tell us whether effects last. Thus, follow-up assessments are generally of greater interest to practitioners and policy makers. However, long-term follow-ups (particularly those that follow brief interventions) may communicate unrealistic expectations about the durability of intervention gains. Reviewers should specify the post-treatment and follow-up intervals of interest (e.g., 6 months to 2 or 3 years after the end of treatment).

In Chapter 5 we will consider how to handle multiple measures on a single construct, multiple sources of information on a particular outcome measure, and multiple measures of outcomes over time.

Research Designs

Certain designs are superior to others when it comes to answering specific questions (Higgins & Green, 2006). Since meta-analysis can be used to address different kinds of questions, reviewers should establish inclusion criteria that specify designs that can generate credible answers to their central questions. For instance, survey data can be appropriate for reviews of the incidence and prevalence of a condition or disorder. Longitudinal data can be used in syntheses of research on epidemiological or attitudinal change. Reviews of the predictive validity (prognostic accuracy) of instruments that assess the risk of child maltreatment require prospective studies. Reviews of intervention effects rely on studies that address plausible threats to the validity of causal inferences (Shadish, Cook, & Campbell, 2002).

We will focus on designs that are appropriate for meta-analyses on intervention effects for two reasons. First, these "What works?" reviews have been of greatest interest in social work and other helping professions in recent years. Second, appropriate research designs for causal inferences have been hotly debated: how do we know whether outcomes can be attributed to an intervention and not to other causes? Fortunately, there is some evidence in the methodology literature that bears on this debate. In short, variations in study design and quality of implementation are associated with different results. These "method effects" can account for as much of the variation in outcomes as treatment variables (Wilson & Lipsey, 2001) and can lead to wrong conclusions (Deeks et al., 2003).

Randomized controlled trials (RCTs) are considered the "gold standard" for assessing effects of interventions because they control most threats to internal validity (see Shadish, Cook, & Campbell, 2002). Random allocation of participants to treatment conditions creates comparable groups, and when treatment is applied to one group and not another (or different treatments are provided to different groups), investigators can identify treatment effects apart from the influence of other factors. When properly implemented, RCTs are simply the best designs for ruling out rival plausible explanations for results and supporting credible inferences about treatment effects. However, some RCTs do not provide convincing evidence of treatment effects because they are poorly implemented (e.g., allowing violations of initial assignments or mixing treatments across groups) or because differential attrition alters the initial composition of the groups (Shadish, Cook, & Campbell, 2002). In these instances, factors other than treatment may account for between-group differences (or similarities) on outcome measures.

Other designs that aim to provide support for causal inferences include propensity score matching, Heckman selection models, difference-in-differences, regression discontinuity, and interrupted time-series designs (see Shadish, Cook, and Campbell, 2002). Several studies have shown that nonrandomized studies sometimes, but not always, over- or underestimate effects obtained in well-implemented RCTs (Bloom, Michalopoulos, Hill, & Lei, 2002; Deeks et al., 2003; Glazerman, Levy, & Myers, 2002; Kunz & Oxman, 1998; Schultz, Chalmers, Hayes, & Altman, 1995; Schulz & Grimes, 2002; Shadish & Ragsdale, 1996). None of the nonrandomized designs *consistently* over- or underestimates effects across substantive domains. Thus we cannot rely on design features alone to produce reliable estimates. Instead, we must consider plausible threats to validity in the set of studies under investigation. (This has implications for our assessments of study quality, discussed in Chapter 4.)

To illustrate this problem, let us take the example of a Cochrane review on effects of fencing swimming pools to prevent drowning deaths to children (Thompson & Rivara, 1998). The authors found no RCTs on the topic but did find case-control studies that provide compelling evidence that isolation (four-sided) fences with secure latches prevent drowning. The evidence is convincing because there are no other *plausible* explanations (other than fencing) for differences in drowning deaths. Thus, nonrandomized studies *may* provide credible evidence of effects *if* alternative explanations can be ruled out.

Many meta-analyses of treatment include randomized and non-randomized group designs (those in which there is a treatment and a comparison/control group). Some of these designs are better than others. Those that use historical controls (comparisons to groups that were formed in the past) are weaker than studies with concurrent control groups (because recent events and policy changes may create differences between groups). Studies that match groups on characteristics thought to influence outcomes (and those that use propensity score matching) are stronger than groups formed by convenience. Shadish, Cook, and Campbell (2002) provide an excellent discussion of the many possible group designs and their relative strengths and weaknesses. In general, nonrandomized studies are vulnerable to *selection bias*; that is, initial differences between groups in terms of their prognosis may explain between-group differences in outcomes (Larzelere, Kuhn, & Johnson, 2004).

Single-group designs, such as those that use pretests and post-tests (sometimes called before-and-after studies) are vulnerable to many threats to internal validity (e.g., statistical regression, maturation, selection bias, testing effects). These designs and single-subject designs are routinely excluded from systematic reviews and meta-analyses. However, methodologists are working on methods for including single-subject data in meta-analyses (Kendrick et al., 2007; Shadish, 2007).

To a great extent, the question about whether design features matter (and which features matter) in the context of a particular field of inquiry is an empirical problem. Campbell Collaboration reviews can include both randomized and nonrandomized studies, but authors are expected to analyze results separately and test the differences with moderator analysis (Shadish & Myers, 2004). If randomized and nonrandomized studies produce similar (homogeneous) estimates of effect size, one could pool the results. If randomized experiments produce significantly larger or smaller effect sizes than other studies, results of different study designs should be kept separate. For example, Scher and colleagues (2006) concentrated on high-quality RCTs but also examined evidence from nonrandomzied studies. They found that nonrandomized studies produced higher effect sizes than RCTs, which suggests that the former may be upwardly biased.

In sum, there is no single set of design criteria that reviewers can pull off a shelf and use for every systematic review. Rather, analysts should take the following steps:

1. Set a minimum threshold for acceptable designs in the context of a specific review.
2. Carefully assess variations among included studies in study design and implementation characteristics that may increase the risk of bias (see Chapter 4).
3. Use moderator analysis to assess effects of specific design features (as discussed in Chapter 6).

The minimum threshold will depend on the central research question. If this question concerns treatment effects or other topics that involve causal inference, some reviewers will limit included designs to RCTs and assess the risk of bias in these trials (as is often done in Cochrane reviews). In addition to RCTs, other reviewers will include certain parallel cohort designs (e.g., those that use matching or statistical controls for baseline differences between groups), assess the risk of bias in these studies, and see whether results match those of the RCTs. There is no consensus on where to set the bar. This is due, in part, to the fact that designs vary across intervention types. For example, RCTs are more likely to be used with individual treatments than population-based interventions (Ogilvie, Egan, Hamilton, & Petticrew, 2005).

Other Inclusion and Exclusion Criteria

Cultural and Geopolitical Contexts

Cochrane and Campbell reviews aim to provide evidence that is relevant around the world; therefore, their default position is that there should be no geographic inclusion/exclusion criteria unless there are good reasons for them. Geographic boundaries are inescapable in reviews of interventions that exist only in certain parts of the world. For example, it is necessary to limit reviews of effects of the Temporary Assistance for Needy Families (TANF) program to studies conducted in the United States, since that program exists only in the United States. However, welfare (public assistance) and workfare programs exist in many countries (Smedslund et al., 2006).

Interventions that are "exported" from one place to another do not always "travel" well because cultural, social, organizational, and political contexts can greatly shape the implementation and effects of interventions. Therefore, when there is reason to believe that geopolitical contexts affect the implementation or results of an intervention, reviewers might limit a systematic review to similar contexts (e.g., developed or developing nations) or examine contextual differences in moderator analysis.

Language Criteria

Given concerns about language-related publication biases (Egger et al., 1997c), the Cochrane and Campbell Collaborations caution against language restrictions. Searches can be conducted using both English-language and non-English-language terms, but this is rarely done. English search terms will sometimes lead to identification of some non-English-language reports. The decision to impose language criteria has much to do with available personnel and resources. Translation services can be obtained (often through Cochrane's Collaborative Review Groups). Although language restrictions are less than ideal, when they are necessary and well documented, authors can argue that they have provided a clear boundary around the search, which could be extended later by using other language search terms and publications.

Time Frame

It is important to set clear boundaries on the time frame covered by the review. For reviews of well-defined interventions, it may be possible to identify a clear start date, beginning when the intervention was first reported. A clear end date facilitates the process of updating a review, because the update will begin where the previous version left off. Occasionally, reviewers will limit the time frame to certain historical periods. Generally, systematic reviews should include all of the relevant studies, unless there are specific reasons for interest in a particular time frame. These interests might relate to reform movements, major policy shifts, emergence of controversies, or the availability of a new method or instrument (Lipsey & Wilson, 2001).

As with geopolitical contexts, historical changes can have powerful influences on social programs that moderate or mediate their effects. Meta-analysts may use cumulative meta-analysis to see whether intervention effects varied over time (e.g., Gilbody et al., 2006; see Chapter 6). Of course, this requires inclusion of studies conducted during all time periods. Another approach was taken by Smedslund and colleagues (2006), who used moderator analysis to examine the impact of welfare-to-work programs in the United States during the Johnson, Reagan, Ford, G. H. Bush, Clinton, and G. W. Bush administrations (the strongest effects were seen during the Johnson administration).

Publication Type

With the publication of Rothstein, Sutton, and Bornstein's (2005) book devoted to the problem of publication bias in meta-analysis, it is now clear that a systematic review should never use publication status as an inclusion criterion (see also Glasziou et al., 2001; Higgins & Green, 2006; Song et al., 2000). For reasons that are unclear, the pervasive evidence about publication bias has not been fully recognized in the social work literature. For example, in a recent article, Hodge claimed that "the extent to which researchers favour submitting significant findings rather than nonsignificant findings remains unclear" (2007, p. 184). This is simply not true. In fact, Dickersin (2005) shows that the main source of publication bias rests with authors who decide not to submit null results; journal reviewers and editors play a smaller role, although they have in the past shouldered more of the blame for this problem.

Put succinctly, the problem is that published reports are not representative of the research literature as a whole. Published studies are not necessarily of higher quality than unpublished studies (McLeod & Weisz, 2004), and the published literature is biased toward higher effect sizes (Dickersin, 2005; Song et al., 2000). This can exert unwanted influence on the conclusions of narrative reviews as well as meta-analyses. Publication bias is a serious threat to the validity of research reviews. When a review points to overall positive results, we should ask whether this could be an artifact of publication and dissemination biases.

Some reviews have been limited to dissertations as well as published studies. This is not sufficient, since other high-quality studies may be missed, and the missing data may point to different conclusions.

In Chapter 6 we discuss ways to assess and correct for publication bias in meta-analysis. The primary way to avoid publication bias in a systematic review and meta-analysis, however, is to locate both published and unpublished studies. We describe strategies for this in Chapter 3.

Developing a Protocol

Preparing a systematic review and meta-analysis is a complex process that involves many judgments and decisions. The process should be as rigorous and transparent as possible in order to minimize bias. Thus, as in any scientific endeavor, the methods used in a systematic review and meta-analysis should be established beforehand (Higgins & Green, 2006; Sutton et al., 1998). The Cochrane and Campbell Collaborations require reviewers to develop and submit detailed written protocols. These protocols are submitted for peer review, and the final versions are posted in the Cochrane and Campbell Libraries (on the World Wide Web) so that readers can assess these plans and determine whether the review was conducted in accordance with the initial plan.

In this section we discuss several important aspects of protocol development: crafting a title for the proposed review, developing a written protocol, and disclosing conflicts of interest.

Titles for Systematic Reviews and Meta-Analyses

The central focus of the review should be clearly expressed in its title. The Cochrane Collaboration and the QUOROM statement express different conventions for such titles.

Many Cochrane reviews use the following template for reviews of intervention effects: "[intervention] for [condition/problem] in [population]." For example, one Cochrane review is titled "Cognitive-Behavioural Therapy for Anxiety Disorders in Children and Adolescents" (James, Soler, & Weatherall, 2005). For some reviews it is desirable to add phrases that describe the counterfactual (comparison condition), specifying certain contexts (e.g., hospitals, schools, developing countries) and/or indicating which outcomes are of interest. Thus, one could expand the template shown above to "effects of [intervention] compared to [control/comparison condition] for [condition/problem] in [population] in [context] on [outcomes]."

The QUOROM statement suggests that it is important to include the phrase *meta-analysis* (or *systematic review*) in the title of published research syntheses (Moher et al., 1999). This makes it easier for interested readers to locate these works. These keywords are routinely omitted from titles of Cochrane and Campbell reviews because all are systematic reviews and most contain meta-analysis.

Contents of a Protocol

The Cochrane Collaboration has developed an excellent standard format for protocols for systematic reviews and meta-analyses of intervention effects (Higgins & Green, 2006; also see National Health Service Centre for Reviews and Dissemination, 2001). The protocol consists of the following:

- a cover sheet with the title, citation details, and contact information for authors;
- an introduction (background and statement of objectives);
- methods:
  - study eligibility criteria,
  - search methods (databases, keyword strings, gray literature strategies),
  - data extraction (coding sheets, quality assessment, plans for reliability checks), and
  - data analysis and synthesis (plans for meta-analysis, subgroup and moderator analysis, publication bias, sensitivity analysis, etc.);
- acknowledgements and conflicts of interest;
- tables and figures relevant to the background or methods; and
- references.

The Cochrane Collaboration's Review Manager (RevMan) software (described in Appendix B) includes an outline for protocols that is easily expanded to produce a full report on a completed systematic review and meta-analysis. Appendix C provides a more detailed outline for protocols and reports on systematic reviews and meta-analyses. The main point here is that plans for analysis should be laid out in advance. This includes deciding which meta-analytic models and methods are likely to be appropriate and what subgroups and moderators will be examined (see Chapters 5 and 6). The peer-review process can be very helpful in this regard.

Conflicts of Interest

Potential conflicts of interest and sponsorship arrangements should be disclosed in the protocol, because these issues can affect reviewers' conclusions (Higgins & Green, 2006; Jørgensen, Hilden, & Gøtzsche, 2006; Lexchin, Bero, Djulbegovic, & Clark, 2003). Potential conflicts of interest include financial or other ties to an intervention under review, involvement in the conduct of one or more studies under review, and publication of a previous review on the same topic.

When Plans Change

Although every effort is made to create a detailed protocol that can act as a guide for the systematic review and meta-analysis, reviewers may encounter unexpected difficulties and craft better strategies than they had initially envisioned. If changes are made, the review authors are required to explain what plans were changed and why. As one can see, the goal of transparency is important in conducting systematic reviews.

Conclusion

There are many important issues to consider when planning a systematic review and meta-analysis. A review team requires diverse knowledge and skills, including understanding of relevant substantive issues, information technology, and methods of research synthesis. Reviewers should think about how and when they will involve consumers, practitioners, and policy makers in discussions about the objectives and scope of a systematic review. It is best to involve some of these "end users" in the planning stages to insure the review's relevance for practice and policy.

   Systematic reviews require a strong conceptual framework. Reviewers articulate their objectives, formulate clear questions or hypotheses, and develop specific eligibility criteria for the review. Eligibility criteria determine the populations, interventions, comparisons, outcomes, and research designs that will and will not be included in the review. Additional criteria may specify the geopolitical and cultural boundaries and time frames covered.

Reviewers write a formal title and protocol for the review to express their intentions. The protocol details the methods that will be used to identify, assess, and synthesize information. Potential conflicts of interests are also described in the protocol.

Main Points: Chapter 2

- Review teams require diverse perspectives and skills, including knowledge of the substantive area, information technology, and methods of research synthesis.
- Input from practitioners, policy makers, and consumers is useful in planning a review.
- Reviewers should formulate specific, clear, answerable questions (or hypotheses) to guide the review.
- Logic models use a diagram format to illustrate hypothesized relationships between key concepts. These models are helpful for identifying central questions and setting the parameters of a systematic review.
- Eligibility criteria specify the study designs, populations, interventions, comparisons, and outcome measures that will be included in the review.
- Additional eligibility criteria may include geopolitical or cultural limitations and time frames. Publication status should not be an eligibility criterion.
- A formal title and detailed protocol (plan) for the review are developed in advance.
- The protocol specifies the objectives of a review, eligibility criteria, and methods that will be used to identify, analyze, and synthesize data. The protocol also includes a statement of potential conflicts of interest.

- If changes in the protocol are needed later, reviewers explain what was changed and why.

For Further Reading

Cooper, H., Hedges, L., & Valentine, J. (forthcoming). *Handbook of research synthesis* (2nd ed.). New York: Russell Sage Foundation.

Higgins, J. P. T., & Green, S. (Eds.) (2006). *Cochrane handbook for systematic reviews of interventions.* Chichester, UK: John Wiley & Sons. Retrieved July 11, 2007, from http://www.cochrane.org/resources/handbook/.

Rothstein, H., Sutton, A. J., & Bornstein, M. (Eds.). (2005). *Publication bias in meta-analysis: Prevention, assessment, and adjustments.* Chichester, UK: Wiley.

3

Locating and Screening Studies

Systematic reviews and meta-analyses are observational studies based on available results from prior studies. It is important to think about how studies and their results are located and included in a review. This is essentially a sampling problem, and the issues are similar to those that arise in sampling individuals or households in social surveys: we identify a population of interest and try to obtain a sample of subjects that represents that population.

From the universe of all potentially relevant studies for a review—that is, all of the studies we would like to have to provide full information on our topic—we are likely to have access to only a sample. What is the nature of that sample? Some studies that bear on our topic will not have been conducted, others are still in progress, and some completed studies will be difficult to locate. To obtain a representative sample and avoid the "file drawer problem" (publication bias and related biases), it is important to invest extra effort in obtaining the fugitive or "gray" literature.

Our universe of relevant studies may have important characteristics that would lead us to think about stratifying the sample. We may want to know about the effects of an intervention that has been implemented in different contexts and with different subgroups of clients. Will we be able to obtain good (large, representative) samples in each of the strata (contexts, populations)? For example, if we want to assess effects of Multisystemic Therapy for youth in the juvenile justice, child welfare, and mental health systems, we will find several studies in juvenile justice and relatively few in the other service sectors. Thus, the available sample of studies does not adequately represent the universe of potentially relevant studies. Similarly, we want to find studies conducted by program developers and by independent investigators to identify allegiance effects (Luborsky et al., 1999), but there are relatively few studies in the latter group (Littell, Popa, & Forsythe, 2005).

To map the universe of potentially relevant studies, some investigators develop *scoping reviews* or *systematic maps* of a body of research before undertaking a systematic review. Scoping reviews provide an overview of the number and types of studies that have been conducted on a broad topic. Systematic maps identify and categorize studies, using generic keywords to describe the study, population, setting, and design. Bates and Coren (2006) compiled a systematic map of literature on the extent and impact of parental mental health problems on the family; available interventions; and the acceptability, accessibility, and effectiveness of interventions.

From the relevant studies that are located for a review and meta-analysis, we may have access to only a subset of the results. This problem is illustrated in Figure 3.1. There are many possible reasons for missing data in the primary studies. Some participants drop out of treatment; others refuse to answer research questions. Some outcome measures do not hold up well in the field and, as a result of concerns about their validity, may not be reported by investigators. Selective reporting on subgroups and/or on some outcomes and not others are additional possible reasons for missing data.

All of these issues affect the external validity of a review—that is, what kinds of generalizations we can make based on available data. Reviewers should try to answer two questions in this regard. First, to what extent are included studies representative of the universe of all

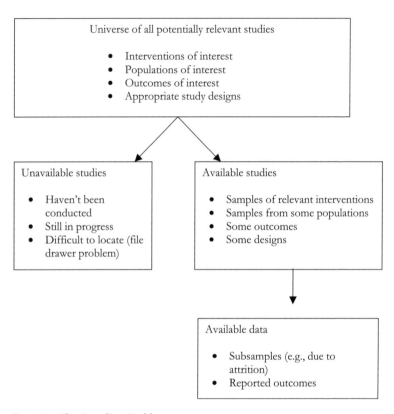

Figure 3.1. The Sampling Problem.

potentially relevant studies? For example, are available studies conducted only in certain settings (e.g., university clinics, community-based agencies, or private practice)? Second, to what extent are included data representative of results of actual studies?

Basic principles of sampling (and probability theory) tell us that convenience samples are not likely to be representative of larger populations of interest. Thus, a convenience sample of studies (those that you read, liked, and saved over the past few years, or those that are located in a single keyword search in PsycINFO) are not going to capture the full range of studies needed in a meta-analysis. A variety of sources and strategies are needed to locate all potentially relevant studies.

The Search Process

As noted earlier, librarians and information retrieval specialists should be consulted when planning a literature search. The field of information science is developing so rapidly that it is important to utilize experts to identify relevant electronic databases and create search strings (keywords and Boolean operators) that will produce sensitive and specific (efficient) searches in those databases. Information scientists can also help researchers document the search process so that it will be transparent and replicable (Patrick et al., 2004). Some information scientists will help you conduct the searches and retrieve documents. The Cochrane Collaboration and the Campbell Collaboration have well-trained trial search coordinators who are experts at locating relevant information for systematic reviews and meta-analyses. Trial search coordinators are available to design and conduct the searches for systematic reviews that are registered with the collaborations.

Bibliographic Databases

Keyword searches of electronic bibliographic databases are an essential component of any literature search strategy. There is only partial overlap in the contents of different databases. Therefore, since systematic reviews aim to provide a comprehensive summary of the literature, it is important to run electronic searches in multiple databases.

Databases relevant for one review will not necessarily be useful for another. Social work reviews should include searches of Social Work Abstracts, Social Services Abstracts, and Dissertation Abstracts International. Beyond those sources, the selection of relevant databases depends on the topic. PsycINFO, Sociological Abstracts, and MEDLINE/PubMed will be useful for many reviews, as will the Cumulative Index to Nursing and Allied Health Literature (CINAHL) and the Education Resources Information Center (ERIC).

Search Terms and Strings

Search terms are keywords that are looked up in a database. These terms often refer to populations, interventions, comparisons, and outcomes of interest. Symbols (wild cards), such as * or &, are used to expand terms to include different versions of the word. Different wildcard symbols are used in different databases. For example, when entered in PsycINFO, the term adolescen* will expand to adolescent, adolescents, and adolescence. It is important to include synonyms for key search terms; for example, we would use teen* as well as adolescen*. Consult with substantive experts and librarians to identify useful synonyms.

Search strings are generated by combining keywords with the Boolean operators AND, OR, NOT, and, in some databases, NEAR or ADJ (adjacent). For example, a search for literature on teen pregnancy programs might use the string (adolescen* OR teen*) AND pregnan* AND (program* OR service* OR treat* OR interven* OR prevent*). Trial search coordinators, librarians, and other information retrieval specialists can help you identify the correct Boolean operators and string formats for a specific database.

If the literature on a topic is very small, PICO terms (populations, interventions, comparisons, and outcomes) may be all you need. If the literature is large, you may need to narrow the search to empirical evidence on these matters. To do this, add terms such as outcome*, evaluat*, effect*, experiment*, and trial (Lipsey & Wilson, 2001).

A comprehensive search strategy lists specific keywords, strings, and Boolean operators used in each database. An example is provided in Appendix D; this is from the Cochrane and Campbell review of cognitive-behavioral interventions for sexually abused children, by Macdonald, Higgins, and Ramchandani (2006).

Hand Searching

To find relevant studies that are not properly indexed in electronic databases, hand searching of the contents of relevant journals is often required (Hopewell, Clarke, Lefebvre, & Scherer, 2006). This involves identifying highly relevant journals and conducting a manual, page-by-page search of their entire contents looking for potentially eligible studies. This is necessary because some articles are not included in electronic bibliographic databases, and those that are may have titles and abstracts that are insufficient for identifying eligible studies (Higgins & Green, 2006). Hand searching is a very time-consuming task, but the Cochrane Collaboration has organized a massive effort to hand-search medical journals while avoiding duplication of effort.

Sources of Gray Literature

Sometimes referred to as the fugitive literature, gray literature is produced at "all levels of government, academia, business and industry in print and electronic formats, but [is] not controlled by commercial publishers" (Hopewell, Clarke, & Mallett, 2005, p. 49). Some unpublished studies can be located in Dissertation Abstracts International, ERIC (published conference proceedings), and other conference proceedings (e.g., abstracts published in connection with meetings of the Society for Social Work and Research, American Psychological Association, or Association for Policy Analysis and Management). The Social Sciences Citation Index includes conference abstracts. Public Affairs Information Service (PAIS) includes government publications and other gray literature sources. Government and research organizations such as those listed above are also good sources of unpublished studies. News on the Open-SIGLE database (System for Information on Gray Literature) is available at international.inist.fr/article55 .html.

The Cochrane Collaboration's CENTRAL database contains information on many trials in health care (see www.cochrane.org and www .mrw.interscience.wiley.com/cochrane/), as do the U.S. National Institutes of Health (NIH) Computer Retrieval of Information on Scientific Projects (CRISP) database (crisp.cit.nih.gov), www.ClinicalTrials .gov, and Current Controlled Trials (www.controlled-trials.com).

Additional studies may be located by searching Web sites maintained by state, national, and international organizations that have commissioned, conducted, or collected studies in your topic area. Consider searching Web sites for the following types of organizations:

- government agencies (e.g., U.S. Centers for Disease Control & Prevention, General Accounting Office, and National Institutes of Health; U.K. Home Office, Economic & Social Research Council);
- research organizations (e.g., ABT Associates, American Institutes for Research, Child Trends, EPPI-Center, Mathematica Policy Research, MDRC, Rand Corporation, SCIE, Urban Institute, Westat Inc.);
- foundations (e.g., Annie E. Casey, Ford, Robert Wood Johnson, Rockefeller); and/or
- archives and clearinghouses (e.g., U.S. National Clearinghouse on Child Abuse and Neglect Information, What Works Clearinghouse; U.K. Economic & Social Data Service)

Other sources are listed by Hopewell, Clarke and Mallett (2005) and Petticrew and Roberts (2006).

A general Web search can be performed using keywords and any search engine (e.g., Google or Yahoo), but be prepared to sift through many hits.

Personal Contacts and Listservs

An additional way to find gray literature is to contact people who are experts in the area. Program developers, principal investigators, and other meta-analysts may have collections of unpublished material and work in progress. We have used a snowball sampling technique to identify and tap these sources. We ask each expert to review our current list of studies and identify potentially eligible studies that are missing from the list. We also ask experts to name other key informants who might have relevant information, and then we follow each of those leads. Many reviewers post requests for information to relevant Listservs (e.g., Child Maltreatment Researchers List). Be sure to keep copies of all correspondence to document these aspects of the search. A brief summary of contacts is often included in reports on systematic reviews.

Reference Harvesting

Previous reviews of the literature are useful places to find potentially relevant references. Scanning the reference lists in these sources is a good way to identify studies that might have been missed in an electronic search. Papers that are in press and unpublished studies are often located this way. These new references are then "harvested" and added to the growing collection of potentially eligible sources.

Some reviews can be located by typing in topic search terms and crossing them with the term "review." Dissertations are another good source, as they tend to include a comprehensive review of the literature pertaining to the research topic. Previous systematic reviews can be located in the Cochrane Database of Systematic Reviews (www.cochrane.org), the Campbell Collaboration C2-RIPE Library (www.campbellcollaboration.org), and the Database of Abstracts of Reviews of Effect (DARE) maintained by the Centre for Reviews and Dissemination at the University of York (www.york.ac.uk/inst/crd/crddatabases.htm).

Documenting the Search

For each database and site searched, you should record the date the search was undertaken, the name or initials of the person who ran the search, the title of the database, the name of the host or portal, the range of dates (earliest and latest dates) covered in the database or any date restrictions placed on the search, the number of hits, and the results. Also record information on hand searches (names of journals searched, dates covered), personal contacts (names and dates), and so forth. This makes the search replicable and provides a clear starting point for later updates. The *Cochrane Handbook* provides examples of search strategies and ways to document different aspects of the search process.

Data Management

You can download results of electronic searches (citations and abstracts) into reference software programs, such as Endnote, Procite, and Reference Manager (RefMan). Automatic downloads are very efficient, as they allow you to skip the laborious step of typing citations. Further, the reference software can be used when screening titles and abstracts for inclusion in meta-analysis (the next step) and for citing included and excluded studies in the final report.

Screening and Eligibility Decisions

Once references are obtained, they must be screened to see which are relevant according to our inclusion and exclusion criteria (discussed in Chapter 2).

Screening and Retrieval Decisions

Sometimes references that are clearly irrelevant can be excluded based on their title alone, but it is best to read the abstract if there is any doubt. If uncertainty remains after reading the abstract, the full text of the report should be obtained.

Decisions about screening and full-text retrieval should be made by more than one person. Most reviewers use inclusive criteria for screening and retrieval decisions—that is, after two people read the titles and abstracts independently, full-text reports are obtained for all of the citations that *either* reader thinks are potentially relevant.

Eligibility Decisions

Once a set of citations has passed the initial screening and full-text reports are available, study eligibility decisions are made by two or more independent raters. Working independently, they read the full text carefully, decide whether the study should be included or excluded, and document reasons for their decisions. Then they compare notes and resolve differences, sometimes with the help of a third reader (Higgins & Green, 2006). It may be necessary to obtain additional information on a study from the principal investigators before the team can determine whether the study should be included in the review. Cochrane reviews list studies in this category as "awaiting assessment" until additional information is available.

Studies should not be ruled out if they do not report an outcome of interest, nor should they be omitted if reported data do not permit effect size calculations. Those data might be obtained from the original investigators. Given concerns about outcome reporting bias (Chan et al., 2004), it is important to try to obtain unpublished data on outcomes of interest. To identify and minimize outcome reporting bias, reviewers should attempt to obtain *all* available reports (both published and unpublished) on eligible studies. Some investigators will also provide access to the raw data.

Inclusion and exclusion criteria are established in advance of the search, but sometimes we encounter studies that raise issues not yet considered. This may lead us to refine the original criteria. If that happens, the new criteria should be applied to all citations previously screened. Reviewers are obliged to show that the changes in study inclusion or exclusion criteria did not alter results of the review (sensitivity analysis can be used for this purpose, as described in Chapter 6).

Tracking Citations and Procurement Status

It is important to track the status of each citation identified in the search. There are several ways to do this. Notes can be placed in the reference software that contains citations, but this has limited utility. References can be exported into a spreadsheet or database for tracking purposes. We have exported citations from Endnote into Excel, where we track their sources, procurement status, and screening and eligibility decisions. Source fields indicate where the reference was located (including names of specific databases, Web sites, and personal contacts). Procurement status fields are flags that indicate whether the abstract is available, whether the full text has been requested (when, by whom, and from what source), and whether the full text has been obtained. We also document specific reasons for exclusion for each citation that has been ruled out (e.g., doesn't meet population criteria, doesn't meet intervention criteria, doesn't meet design criteria).

TrialStat Corporation offers Web-based software, called SRS, to facilitate certain steps in the systematic review: screening of titles and abstracts, establishing interrater agreement on study inclusion and exclusion decisions, and extracting data from included studies. Citations can be uploaded into SRS, and PDF or Word copies of full-text reports can be attached to citations. Reviewers are assigned to sets of citations. The program allows reviewers to establish different levels of screening, eligibility decisions, and coding of data from primary studies. κ estimates are produced to evaluate agreement between pairs of reviewers. EPPI-Reviewer is another Web-based program used to manage many stages of the review process, including citation management, screening of titles and abstracts, data extraction, and basic meta-analysis.

Duplicate and Multiple Reports

A single citation often appears in multiple databases, so it will be necessary to eliminate exact duplicates from your records. This is easily done in most reference management software with built-in functions to eliminate duplicates.

It is a bit more difficult to identify multiple reports that emanate from a single study. Sometimes these reports will have the same authors, sample sizes, program descriptions, and methodological details. However, author lines and sample sizes may vary, especially when there are reports on subsamples taken from the original study (e.g., preliminary results or special reports). Care must be taken to ensure that we know which reports are based on the same samples or on overlapping samples—in meta-analysis these should be considered multiple reports from a *single* study.

When there are multiple reports on a single study, we put all of the citations for that study together in summary information on the study.

Close examination of all of the reports on a study should promote better understanding of the study methods and results. Inconsistencies between reports are not uncommon; these lead to queries for the original investigators.

Reporting Search and Screening Results

The final report should explicate the search process in detail so that it can be replicated and updated (Patrick et al., 2004). The QUOROM statement indicates that reports on meta-analyses should include a description of the search strategy used "in detail (e.g., databases, registers, personal files, expert informants, agencies, hand-searching), and any restrictions (years considered, publication status, language of publication)" (Moher et al., 1999). This should be accompanied by a QUOROM-type flowchart that illustrates the results of the search process, screening, and study eligibility decisions. An example is provided in Figure 3.2.

Additionally, researchers should provide readers with a complete bibliographic list of excluded studies, with specific reasons for exclusion for each citation and study that is not in the meta-analysis. This list will answer questions about why a particular study wasn't included.

Conclusion

This chapter described systematic strategies for locating studies and procedures used to document the search process. The emphasis has been on the necessity for a comprehensive search that includes multiple databases and sources of studies so that all potentially relevant studies are found and sampling bias is not introduced. In the absence of a careful search for gray literature, publication and dissemination biases pose threats to the validity of a systematic review and meta-analysis.

Also essential are the use of transparent procedures that are carefully executed and documented in detail. This documentation allows readers

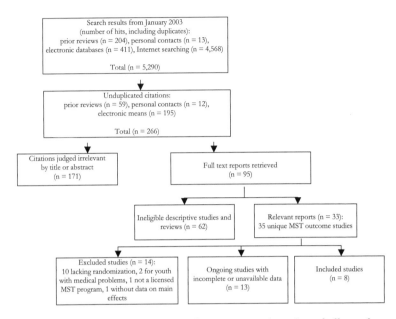

Figure 3.2. QUOROM-type flow chart from a systematic review of effects of Multisystemic Therapy. *Source*: Littell, Popa, & Forsyth, 2005.

to critically appraise the search as to its adequacy. It also facilitates updates and extensions of a search.

After citations and abstracts are screened, eligible studies are identified, and relevant reports are retrieved, data must be extracted from the reports and coded. We will turn to coding procedures in Chapter 4.

Main Points: Chapter 3

- A variety of sources and strategies are needed to locate all potentially relevant studies; consultation with a librarian and information retrieval specialist is essential.
- Keyword searches of electronic bibliographic databases are an important component of any literature search strategy. Keywords often refer to populations, interventions, comparisons, and outcomes of

interest. They are combined with Boolean operators and wildcards in strings that are tailored for particular databases.

- Hand searching (page-by-page examination) of relevant journals is often required to identify articles that are not properly indexed or are inadequately described in abstracts.
- The gray literature must also be searched through databases and Web sites, personal contacts, Listservs, government and research organizations, and reference harvesting, especially of dissertations.
- At least two people should screen studies and determine their eligibility for the review.
- Citations should be tracked along with their procurement status, eligibility status, and specific reasons for exclusion (if applicable).

For Further Reading

Higgins, J. P. T., & Green, S. (Eds.) (2006). *Cochrane handbook for systematic reviews of interventions.* Chichester, UK: John Wiley & Sons.

Hopewell, S., Clarke, M., & Mallett, S. (2005). Grey literature and systematic reviews. In H. R. Rothstein, A. J. Sutton, & M. Bornstein (Eds.), *Publication bias in meta-analysis: Prevention, assessment and adjustments* (pp. 49–72). West Sussex, England: John Wiley & Sons.

Petticrew, M., & Roberts, H. (2006). *Systematic reviews in the social sciences: A practical guide.* Oxford, UK: Blackwell Publishing.

4

Data Extraction and Study
Quality Assessment

Raters extract data from study reports onto paper or electronic coding forms. The data forms provide a bridge between the primary research studies and the research synthesis and serve as a historical record of reviewers' decisions (Higgins & Green, 2006). Data forms capture identifying information on studies, descriptions of interventions, sample characteristics, research methods, outcome measures, and the raw data and statistical information needed to calculate effect sizes.

In this chapter, we discuss data extraction methods and delineate the types of data that should be extracted and coded for further analysis and meta-analysis. We discuss coding procedures, as well as how to train coders and assess reliability in coding. Special attention is paid to the problem of study quality assessment—that is, how we identify variations in quality among the studies included in a systematic review and meta-analysis.

Format and Structure

Coding forms can be paper or electronic. Typically, data entered on paper are reentered in some electronic form, so paper forms add an extra step. On the other hand, paper forms can be easier to set up and modify, which is useful when coding procedures are being developed and pilot-tested. Several software programs can be used for data extraction. Some meta-analysts use spreadsheet software (e.g., Excel), preferably with data entry screens to structure the process. Database programs, such as Access and FoxPro, and specialized programs such as EPPI-Reviewer and TrialStat SRS (described in Appendix B) can also be tailored to structure data extraction for a particular review and meta-analysis. These programs capture categorical and continuous data, along with free text, and can produce reports on extracted data.

Studies typically produce a hierarchical data structure that should be mirrored in the data extraction process—that is, single studies may produce multiple reports, each report usually describes multiple outcome measures, and data on outcome measures may be collected at several points in time. Inevitably, the structure of data reports will vary for different studies. One study might produce a report on preliminary findings, followed by a report on post-treatment results, and then a follow-up study. Another study might produce three or four reports, each dealing with outcomes in different domains.

While it might seem obvious at first, we need to be clear about what constitutes a "study." Usually a study is defined as an investigation that produces one or more reports on a sample that does not overlap with other samples. Thus, in meta-analysis, "studies" are investigations of nonoverlapping samples. This has important implications for data analysis, which we take up in Chapter 5. Briefly, the effect estimates that are included in a meta-analysis must be independent of one another— that is, each meta-analysis can include only one estimate per sample. A single review can include multiple meta-analyses, however.

ID numbers can be used to keep track of relationships between studies, reports, outcome measures, and data collection waves. For example, we have assigned two-digit ID numbers to studies. Reports have a four-digit ID, with the first two coming from the study. Outcome measures have six-digit IDs, the first two from the study, the next two from the report, and a unique two-digit outcome number. Data collection points can be added as well. Thus, the ID number 01–02–06 represents the sixth outcome mentioned in the second report from the first study.

Occasionally, we find a report that provides data on two or more studies (nonoverlapping samples). We assign it to both studies and track outcomes for each study (sample) separately.

Developing Data Extraction Forms

There is no need to start from scratch when creating data extraction forms. Reviewers should first examine the forms used in several rigorous systematic reviews and meta-analyses and then tailor one or more to fit the particular purposes, questions, and substantive topics to be addressed in a new review. A sample data extraction form is provided in Appendix E. Many other examples can be found in appendices of Cochrane and Campbell reviews, and in appendices provided by Lipsey and Wilson (2001) and Petticrew and Roberts (2006).

To the extent possible, coding structures should be established in advance, then pilot-tested by entering data on several studies, and revised as necessary. We may later encounter a study that provides information that does not fit into existing categories; if it is important, we may decide to refine the category scheme. However, this means that we must return to the studies already coded and see whether those codes need to be adjusted. For this reason, it is always useful to leave room on the coding sheets for raters' comments and page numbers where the information can be found in the original reports.

Contents of Data Extraction Forms

As shown in Appendix E, most data extraction forms have several sections, beginning with identifying information on the study and the report. It is important to record the coder's initials and the date on these forms, because you will compare results from different coders. The main sections of data extraction forms are described below.

Study Design and Research Methods

Detailed information on allocation methods, attrition, assessment, and analysis is generally more useful than overall study design codes. One reason for this is that the terms used to describe research designs are not consistent across disciplines. Further, study designs will be limited by the inclusion criteria developed earlier (see Chapter 2). Coding should focus on variations in design features among included studies. We will return to this topic later in this chapter, when we discuss study quality assessment. This section should capture information on the creation of treatment and comparison groups (allocation methods), and the flow of cases through the study. It is important to know when and why subjects were lost. To do that, we try to record how many cases were referred to the study, consented to participate, started treatment (in each group), completed treatment, provided data, and were lost to follow-up. Drop-out and attrition occur for many reasons, and it is essential to understand this. The CONSORT statement (Moher, Schulz, & Altman, 2001; www.consort-statement.org/) provides a good model for reporting case flow through a randomized experiment; it has been adopted as the standard for reporting trials in medicine and in journals of the American Psychological Association. Similar statements are available to guide reporting on nonrandomized trials (TREND; Caetano, 2004) and observational studies (MOOSE; Stroup et al., 2000).

It is important to record information on the unit of random assignment and the unit of analysis. In general, these units should be identical. In *cluster-randomized trials* people are randomly assigned to conditions in groups. The groups may be families, classrooms, agencies, or any social unit. Analysis of cluster-randomized trials often proceeds as if individuals had been randomly assigned. This is a mistake, because observations within clusters are not independent. The "unit of analysis error" can produce false-positive results. The data can be analyzed at the cluster level, but that limits statistical power. Appropriate statistical methods for analyzing clustered data are available; these include multilevel models, variance components analysis, and generalized estimating equations. When you encounter cluster-randomized trials, you might want to check with a statistician to see whether results have been properly analyzed. If not, adjustments will be needed. To prepare for this, you can record information on the number of clusters and/or average size of the clusters and intraclass correlation coefficients (measures of variability within and between clusters) if this is available. In Chapter 5 we discuss the use of intraclass correlation coefficients to obtain accurate effect sizes for cluster-randomized trials.

Interventions

Information on interventions provided to each treatment and control or comparison group is captured here. Usually, separate sections are used to describe treatments received by different groups.

Relevant information includes any available data on the amount (duration, intensity, and frequency) of contact between clients and service providers, along with descriptions of their activities. Treatment modalities are described here (e.g., individual counseling, group work, in-home services, residential treatment). This is also the place to put information on theoretical orientations, reliance on treatment manuals, and any observations about treatment implementation (successes or problems) and fidelity to a reference treatment.

Typically, reviewers capture information on characteristics of service providers, such as their educational background, fields of study, years of experience, and demographic variables. The type and frequency of supervision may be important as well.

Participant Characteristics

Demographic characteristics of participants, such as age, gender, ethnicity, socioeconomic status, and location, are delineated here, along with information on presenting problems.

Outcome Measures

For each outcome measure of interest, we need to record the name of the instrument or method used to obtain data, as well as any available information on the reliability and validity of this method as it was used in the study sample. We also want to know who provided data (e.g., a child, parent, clinician, teacher) and how data were obtained (self-administered survey, interview, administrative data).

We also need to know how the measure was scored and whether a high score means improvement or increased problem severity; or, if the measure captures an event, we need to know whether the event is viewed as a positive or negative outcome. Some reviewers will adjust the polarity of outcome measures so that high scores and events always represent desirable outcomes. This can be confusing to readers who are familiar with the measurement instruments. We prefer to leave the direction of measures alone and take care to describe the results accurately and label graphs appropriately (e.g., Cochrane's RevMan software allows reviewers to indicate which direction favors the treatment group).

Appendix E (Level 4) shows tables used to extract data on outcome measures.

Statistical Information Needed to Calculate Effect Sizes

It is important to record valid N's for each treatment and control/comparison group on each outcome and at each data collection point. These N's may vary across outcomes and over time, with missing data on some participants.

To calculate effect sizes for continuous measures (scales, numeric data), we will need means, standard deviations, and valid N's for each treatment and control or comparison group. Also record all information on statistics used to test for differences between groups (e.g., t-test, F statistic, p values), especially if any of the raw data (means and standard deviations) are not available.

Effect sizes for dichotomous data require information on the number of treatment cases that experienced an event and the number of control cases that experienced the event, along with total valid N's for each group. Again, record all information about statistical tests for differences between groups (e.g., χ^2, df, p value).

Study Quality Assessment

As explained in Chapter 2, most systematic reviews set inclusion criteria that specify which study designs can provide credible answers to the review's central questions. Once these threshold criteria are in place, the purpose of study quality assessment is to capture and analyze *variations* among the included studies—those that met initial inclusion criteria—in terms of their credibility and vulnerability to various sources of bias.

There are several approaches to study quality assessment and a substantial body of work on this topic in the methodology literature (for reviews, see Deeks et al., 2003; Jüni, Altman, & Egger, 2001; Jüni, Witschi, Bloch, & Egger, 1999; Wells & Littell, 2007; Wortman, 1994). Some authors have defined study quality in terms of overall research designs, invoking familiar design hierarchies that place randomized controlled trials (RCTs) at the pinnacle. This is problematic for two reasons. First, RCTs are appropriate for some research questions and not others (e.g., they are not appropriate for meta-analyses on epidemiological or correlational questions). Second, as discussed in Chapter 2, some RCTs "go bad" in the field and do not support credible inferences about intervention effects. Hence, design hierarchies don't resolve questions of credibility and bias. Even when a review is limited to RCTs, a deeper assessment is needed to judge variations in the quality of those studies that may be associated with bias.

A second approach, perhaps the one most often used in meta-analyses that appear in social work journals, involves the use of multiple-item scales to rate overall study quality. For example, the Methodological Quality Rating Scale (MQRS; Miller & Wilbourne, 2002) has been adapted for use in a number of meta-analyses. Like many other scales developed for this purpose, the MQRS contains items that tap different aspects of study quality: overall design, attrition, duration of follow-ups, types of outcome measures (e.g., use of collateral reports), and intervention quality control. The MQRS has 12 items that produce a score ranging from 0 to 17.

Deeks and colleagues (2003) identified 194 similar tools that could be or had been used to assess the quality of nonrandomized studies. Approximately half were scales. Most were "poorly developed with scant attention paid to principles of scale development" (p. ix). The MQRS was ranked among the top 14 tools rated but was not considered suitable for use in systematic reviews. Only six tools were considered potentially suitable for such use, but all would require modifications (Deeks et al., 2003).

The main problem with these scales is that they tap study qualities that relate to different types of validity (internal, external, statistical conclusion, and construct validity). Composite scores conflate different aspects of research design with sample size, measurement reliability, and the duration of follow-up. While each of these features may be associated with bias, those biases may work in similar or opposite directions. By conflating different qualities associated with biases of different kinds, we don't have stable measures of "quality" or bias. For example, non-randomized studies may over- or underestimate effects (Glazerman, Levy, & Myers, 2002). Differential attrition can also lead to over- or underestimated effects. Thus, a scale that conflates design with attrition makes it impossible to tell which quality matters and how biases operate in this context. This is an "apples and oranges" problem—mixing different constructs—that can be solved only by keeping design qualities separate and examining their potential effects individually.

Herbison, Hay-Smith, and Gillespie (2006) applied scores from 43 different study quality scales to all of the studies included in 65 meta-analyses contained in 18 systematic reviews. None of the quality scores reliably sorted studies into high- and low-quality groups. They concluded that "it is a mistake to assign meaning to a quality score" (p. 1249) and that the practice of using overall quality scales in meta-analysis should be abandoned.

There is consensus among methodologists and meta-analysts that study qualities should be assessed individually rather than being summed into total quality scores (Higgins & Green, 2006; Shadish & Myers, 2004). The impact of specific study qualities can then be examined in moderator analysis and meta-regression to assess the potential sources of bias and their influence in a set of studies. Which methodological qualities matter and how they affect results can vary, depending on the topic and field of inquiry. We return to this issue in Chapter 6.

The approach taken by the Cochrane and Campbell Collaborations, and the one we recommend here, is to focus on specific study design and implementation issues that may result in bias in the studies included in a particular review. The *Cochrane Handbook* recommends that reviewers assess the following types of bias that may be present in randomized or nonrandomized trials:

- *Selection bias:* systematic differences in the initial composition of groups (e.g., symptom severity, motivation)
- *Performance bias:* systematic differences in the care provided to groups apart from the interventions under investigation (e.g., contamination of treatment)
- *Attrition bias:* systematic differences in dropouts and withdrawals that alter initial group composition
- *Detection bias:* systematic differences in outcome assessment (e.g., expectancy effects due to unblinded assessment) (Higgins & Green, 2006)

Smedslund and colleagues (2006) rated studies on these criteria and others; results are shown in Table 4.1. Appendix E (Level 5) shows questions used to obtain ratings on these criteria in a review by Littell, Campbell, Green, and Toews (2007).

Table 4.1. Quality Coding of Work Programs for Welfare Recipients

Quality Indicators	Met %	Met (N)	Unclear %	Unclear (N)	Not Met %	Not Met (N)
Random generation of allocation	19	(11)	78	(45)	3	(2)
Allocation concealment	28	(16)	72	(42)	0	(0)
Prevention of performance bias	36	(21)	47	(27)	17	(10)
Prevention of detection bias	84	(49)	16	(9)	0	(0)
Prevention of attrition bias	59	(34)	31	(18)	10	(6)
Intention to treat	50	(29)	48	(28)	2	(1)

58 sites; *Source:* Smedslund et al., 2006.

Training Coders

The data extraction process is demanding. It requires coders to reliably pull complex information out of reports that are often less than clear and then fit it into predefined categories. An understanding of research methodology is needed to accomplish this task, and most meta-analysts think that coders should have some doctoral-level training in research methods and statistics. Some authors have found able coders among master's-level students in research classes, but Cochrane Collaboration review groups have had very uneven experiences with master's-level coders.

Here are some simple steps for training coders.

1. Discuss basics of meta-analysis.
2. Have coders read a rigorous meta-analysis and identify inclusion criteria, sample characteristics, main results, results of moderator analysis, and limitations.
3. Explain data extraction processes and coding forms.
4. Have coders read one primary study and extract data from it.
5. Discuss discrepancies between their coding and the master coding.
6. Have two coders extract data from each study and match with the principal investigator's coding. Resolve any discrepancies.

Reliability of Coding

Coding discrepancies will arise when we extract specific information from studies whose methods of presentation may be dissimilar from each other or ambiguous. Given the difficulty of this task, it is better to have two raters code each study independently and then resolve discrepancies rather than rely on a single, unexamined set of codes. In the past, some authors have suggested that reviewers might double-code only a sample of studies, or have one person code the studies on two separate occasions. Because coding requires subjective judgments and difficult interpretations of complex texts, it is always best to have two different people code every study.

Various options have been posed for assessing and reporting reliability. The percentage of initial agreement between coders is sometimes reported, but this is not as useful as a measure of agreement that has been adjusted for chance, such as Cohen's κ (for categorical variables) or the intraclass correlation coefficient (for continuous measures). Generally, we report levels of agreement before a consensus rating is developed to indicate how easy or difficult it was to achieve agreement on coding. There is no standard level for initial reliability (Higgins & Green, 2006), perhaps because raters move on to achieve consensus.

It is important to preserve the initial coding sheets so that information on initial reliability is retained. To record consensus ratings, a duplicate can be made of one initial set of codes and then altered to reflect the consensus ratings.

Missing Data

We noted in the previous chapter that study reports do not always provide the information needed to determine whether the study meets inclusion criteria. When this happens, we ask principal investigators for additional information. Once coders have extracted data from included studies, they are likely to find more pieces of information that are missing. As before, it is important to obtain missing data from principal investigators in order to characterize studies as completely and fairly as possible. After coding, we often have a set of queries for investigators. In our experience, some researchers are very willing to answer questions about their work and provide additional information; others are not as willing or able to do so.

Conclusion

This chapter detailed the procedures used to extract and code data from included studies. Accurate data extraction is necessary to describe study design features and research methods, interventions, participants, and outcome measures. In addition, data extraction provides information necessary to formulate effect sizes and assess the qualities of included studies. One can see the necessity of a team approach in data extraction given the attention required to detailed aspects of the study. Now that we have discussed how to set up a systematic review, search for primary studies, and code them, we will turn, in the next two chapters, to the statistical techniques used in meta-analysis.

Main Points: Chapter 4

- Data extraction forms can be created in a variety of formats. Reviewers should consider adapting forms that have been used in previous reviews.
- Data extraction typically follows a hierarchical structure that allows for multiple reports per study, multiple outcomes per report, and multiple outcomes per report.
- The unit of analysis in a systematic review is the study. Meta-analysis requires independent effect sizes (those from samples that do not overlap with other samples in the analysis).
- Data extraction forms capture identifying information on studies, intervention characteristics, sample characteristics, research design and implementation issues (information needed to assess study quality), outcome measures, timing of data collection, and raw data and statistical information needed to calculate effect sizes.
- Forms must be pilot-tested to make sure that they serve the purposes of a particular review.
- Study quality assessment focuses on specific design features and the risk of selection bias, performance bias, attrition bias, and detection bias. Overall study quality scales should not be used.
- Coding is a detailed and demanding process that requires training. At least two coders independently extract data from each study. Reliability is assessed and consensus ratings are developed by resolving discrepancies between coders.

For Further Reading

Higgins, J. P. T., & Green, S. (Eds.) (2006). *Cochrane handbook for systematic reviews of interventions.* Chichester, UK: John Wiley & Sons. Retrieved July 11, 2007, from http://www.cochrane.org/resources/handbook/.

Lipsey, M. W., & Wilson, D. B. (2001). *Practical meta-analysis.* Thousand Oaks: SAGE Publications.

5

Effect Size Metrics and Pooling Methods

In this chapter we explicate the basic concepts and logic of meta-analysis. We explain the concept of effect size (ES) and describe different types and uses of ESs. We show how ESs are used to understand results of individual studies and provide the basis for meaningful syntheses of results across studies. We discuss the use of ESs as point estimates and the use of confidence intervals to assess the precision of ES estimates. We use graphs called Forest plots to illustrate these ideas.

Later portions of the chapter deal with methods used to combine (pool) ESs across studies to obtain estimates of average effects. In preparation for this, we note that combined effects must be derived from independent estimates. We consider ways to avoid dependencies in meta-analysis. This involves developing strategies for handling multiple groups, measures, data sources, and points in time.

Pooling data across studies is the purpose of meta-analysis. We discuss the concept of weighting study results to achieve more accurate overall estimates. We consider questions about the consistency of ESs across studies, along with different models for combining these results.

Throughout the chapter, we attend to the interpretation of ESs and other products of meta-analysis. We consider how results of meta-analysis can be translated into metrics that are more easily understood by practitioners and policy makers.

Effect Sizes

An *effect size* is a measure of the strength (magnitude) and direction of a relationship between variables. Theoretically, any metric can be used as an ES as long as it is takes into account the magnitude and direction of a relationship, can be expressed as a point estimate with confidence intervals, and provides estimates that are comparable across studies. Most ES metrics fall into three main categories, related to proportions, means, and correlation coefficients. There are several ways to calculate and express ES within each of these categories. We will concentrate on the ES statistics most commonly used in systematic reviews and meta-analyses. Lipsey and Wilson (2001) provide more comprehensive treatment of the variety of ES measures available.

The choice of ES measures is influenced by the purpose and design of a study and the format of the data. Studies that test intervention effects and other kinds of causal inferences typically report differences (e.g., between pre-tests and post-tests, or between treated and untreated groups) in terms of proportions or average scores. Studies that assess relationships between variables without inferring causal directions are likely to report measures of association (e.g., correlations).

Different ES measures are used for dichotomous and continuous data. *Dichotomous* variables have only two categories and are often used to express the presence or absence of a characteristic or event, such as pregnancy, out-of-home placement, hospitalization, or high school graduation. When dichotomous variables are coded 0 and 1 (0 = absence, 1 = presence of the characteristic or event), they are called *binary* variables. Although each individual can have only one value on these variables, grouped data can be expressed in proportions or rates. For example, although pregnancy is a dichotomous variable, we can calculate the proportion of the women in a group who become pregnant and compare pregnancy rates in different groups.

Continuous variables can take on a range of values that can be expressed on a numeric scale. They are often used in addition to dichotomous variables to express the frequency or duration of outcomes. Examples of continuous outcome variables include number of pregnancies (for each woman), number or length of hospitalizations, days in out-of-home placement, and years of education. Scores on tests or scales are also continuous variables and are commonly used as outcome measures in meta-analysis. For example, achievement tests, depression inventories, and symptom checklists (e.g., the Brief Symptom Inventory) are common continuous outcome measures. We use group data on continuous measures to obtain averages. Average scores can then be compared in several ways: before and after an event or intervention, or between treated and untreated groups.

The grouped data we have considered thus far—proportions and averages—are statistics that come from samples. In many kinds of research, including meta-analysis, we use these statistics to estimate population *parameters*. Viewed from this perspective, these statistics are called *point estimates*, because they provide an estimate of the phenomenon of interest in a larger population. Probability theory tells us that if we collect data from multiple samples, the point estimates from those samples will be distributed around the population parameter. Meta-analysis uses this logic, relying on multiple estimates from different studies to obtain a better picture of the distribution of effects and more precise parameter estimates. However, all estimates are approximate and should be presented with *confidence intervals* (CIs) that express the level of certainty that accompanies the estimate.

Based on sample data, we can calculate a CI that is likely to encompass the population parameter in 95% of all of the samples taken from our population of interest. CIs are calculated from *standard errors* (SEs), which in turn are based on the size of the sample and the amount of within-sample variation. The SE is an expression of the *precision* of an estimate; estimates with small SEs are more precise than those with large SEs. The standard 95% CI encompasses values that range from two SEs below the estimate to two SEs above the estimate. This 95% CI can be thought of as a margin of error. It includes the smallest and largest effect sizes that we would expect to find in almost all (95%) similar samples. When the CI includes the null value, the estimate is not statistically significant. The width of a CI is inversely related to sample size (larger samples have smaller CIs) and directly related to the sample variance (samples with larger variances have larger CIs).

Effect Sizes for Dichotomous Data

In the United States, the most commonly used ES measure for dichotomous data is the *odds ratio* (OR). *Odds* refers to the chance that something will happen compared to the chance that it will not. Thus, if 2 people experience an event and 8 do not, the odds are 2/8 (0.25) that someone in the group of 10 will experience the event. The OR is a comparison of two odds; that is, it is the odds that something will happen in one group compared with the odds that it will happen in the other. Let us add a second group of 10 people and say they are exposed to treatment and the odds of the event of interest in this group are 4/6, or 0.67. Now the OR is expressed as the odds for the intervention group divided by the odds for the comparison group: 4/6 divided by 2/8 = 2.67 (see Table 5.1). This means that the odds of the event in the treatment group are 2.67 times the odds of the event in the control group.

The *risk ratio* (or relative risk, RR) is a similar measure that is somewhat easier to interpret than the OR. It is more commonly used in Eur-

Table 5.1. Effect Sizes for Dichotomous Data (Hypothetical Example)

	Event	No event	Total N	Odds	Risk
Treatment group	4	6	10	4/6 = 0.67	4/10 = 0.40
Control group	2	8	10	2/8 = 0.25	2/10 = 0.20

Odds ratio (OR) = (4/6) / (2/8) = 2.67
Risk ratio (RR) = (4/10) / (2/10) = 2.0
Risk difference (RD) = 0.20
Number needed to treat (NNT) = 1/RD = 5

ope. Like the OR, the RR compares the chance of an event in one group with the chance of that event in another group. Thus, it is another ratio of ratios. However, in statistics *risks are not the same as odds*. The risk is the number of people who experience the event divided by the total number in the group. Thus, the risk in the treated group mentioned above is 4/10 (0.4) and the risk for the control group is 2/10 (0.2). The risk ratio is 0.4 divided by 0.2 (2.0). The risk in the treated group is twice as great as the risk in the control group.

In some ways risk is easier to understand than odds, because risks use the group sample size in the denominator while odds use negative cases in the denominator. Further, risks range from zero to one, while odds range from zero to infinity. Risks can be more easily converted to percentages and probabilities. Table 5.2 shows the relationship between odds and risks. When the odds are 2:1 it means that an event will happen twice for every time that it does not happen. This is equal to a risk of 0.67 (2/3). When the odds are 1:2, the risk is 0.50.

Table 5.2. Odds Are Not Risks

Event	No Event	Odds	Risks
100	1	100.00	0.99
50	1	50.00	0.98
20	1	20.00	0.95
10	1	10.00	0.91
5	1	5.00	0.83
4	1	4.00	0.80
3	1	3.00	0.75
2	1	2.00	0.67
1	1	1.00	0.50
1	2	0.50	0.33
1	3	0.33	0.25
1	4	0.25	0.20
1	5	0.20	0.17
1	10	0.10	0.09
1	20	0.05	0.05
1	50	0.02	0.02
1	100	0.01	0.01

Both ORs and RRs are measures of a *relative* effect. Table 5.3 shows the relationship between ORs and RRs. For both ratios, a value of 1 means that the event is equally likely in both groups. Values below 1 represent reduced odds or risks, while values greater than 1 represent increased odds or risks. The difference between OR and RR is small when events are rare and larger when events are more common. An OR of 2:1 versus 1:2 equals 4, while the RR for the same data is 0.67/0.5, or 2. The risk is twice as likely, and the odds are four times greater. Unfortunately, ORs are often interpreted as if they were RRs. Because ORs produce more extreme values than RRs, this misinterpretation leads readers to overestimate large effects and underestimate small effects (Deeks, Higgins, & Altman, 2006).

Table 5.3. Comparison of Odds Ratios, Risk Ratios, and Risk Differences

Treatment				Control						
Event	No Event	Odds	Risk	Event	No Event	Odds	Risk	OR	RR	RD
10	1	10.00	0.91	1	10	0.10	0.09	100.00	10.00	0.82
9	1	9.00	0.90	1	9	0.11	0.10	81.00	9.00	0.80
8	1	8.00	0.89	1	8	0.13	0.11	64.00	8.00	0.78
7	1	7.00	0.88	1	7	0.14	0.13	49.00	7.00	0.75
6	1	6.00	0.86	1	6	0.17	0.14	36.00	6.00	0.71
5	1	5.00	0.83	1	5	0.20	0.17	25.00	5.00	0.67
4	1	4.00	0.80	1	4	0.25	0.20	16.00	4.00	0.60
3	1	3.00	0.75	1	3	0.33	0.25	9.00	3.00	0.50
2	1	2.00	0.67	1	2	0.50	0.33	4.00	2.00	0.33
1	1	1.00	0.50	1	1	1.00	0.50	1.00	1.00	0.00
1	2	0.50	0.33	2	1	2.00	0.67	0.25	0.50	−0.33
1	3	0.33	0.25	3	1	3.00	0.75	0.11	0.33	−0.50
1	4	0.25	0.20	4	1	4.00	0.80	0.06	0.25	−0.60
1	5	0.20	0.17	5	1	5.00	0.83	0.04	0.20	−0.67
1	6	0.17	0.14	6	1	6.00	0.86	0.03	0.17	−0.71
1	7	0.14	0.13	7	1	7.00	0.88	0.02	0.14	−0.75
1	8	0.13	0.11	8	1	8.00	0.89	0.02	0.13	−0.78
1	9	0.11	0.10	9	1	9.00	0.90	0.01	0.11	−0.80
1	10	0.10	0.09	10	1	10.00	0.91	0.01	0.10	−0.82

OR: odds ratio; RR: risk ratio; RD: risk difference.

A third statistic for reporting dichotomous data is the *risk difference* (RD, also called the absolute risk reduction, ARR). The RD is a measure of *absolute* effect. This is calculated as the risk for the treatment group minus the risk for the control group. For the data in Table 5.1, the risk difference is 0.4 minus 0.2, or 0.2 (or 20%). While its interpretation is straightforward, the limitation of the RD statistic is its insensitivity to base rates. For example, a risk that increases from 50% to 52% may be less important than one that increases from 2% to 4%, although in both instances RD = 0.02.

Finally, the RD can be transformed into another useful metric, the *number needed to treat* (NNT). The NNT denotes the number of people who must be treated in order to obtain one more case with a positive outcome. The NNT is the inverse of the RD (1/RD), so the smaller the RD, the larger the NNT. Using the data in Table 5.1, NNT = 1/0.20 = 5. Thus we need to treat five people to produce one more case with the event of interest. If RD = 0.02, NNT = 50.

Another example will show how the ESs for dichotomous data are related and how they are expressed as point estimates with CIs. Leschied and Cunningham (2002) conducted a randomized experiment to test effects of Multisystemic Therapy (MST) for juvenile offenders in Ontario, Canada; 211 youth were randomly assigned to MST and 198 were assigned to a control group that received treatment as usual (TAU). At 1 year of follow-up, 70 of the MST cases and 63 control cases had

Table 5.4. Effect Sizes for Dichotomous Data on Incarceration at 1-Year Follow-Up (Ontario MST Trials)

	N *with* Event	N *with* No event	*Total* N	*Odds*	*Risk*
Treatment group	70	141	211	0.50	0.33
Control group	63	135	189	0.47	0.32

Odds ratio (OR) = 1.06
Risk ratio (RR) = 1.04
Risk difference (RD) = 0.01

Source: Alison Cunningham, personal communication, 2003.

been incarcerated. Table 5.4 shows that the OR = 1.06, RR = 1.04, and RD = 0.01.

Now we need to use CIs to assess the precision of these estimates. Any statistical software program will produce SEs and CIs. We used RevMan, the Cochrane Collaboration's Review Manager software, to calculate 95% CIs. Results show that the 95% CI for OR is 0.70 to 1.61; for RR, it is 0.79 to 1.38; and for RD, it is −0.08 to 0.10 (see Table 5.5). Since the CIs for OR and RR span the value 1, which represents no difference between groups, and the RD could be positive or negative, we are not confident that MST increases or decreases incarceration. In other words, there is no statistically significant difference between groups in the probability of incarceration. When the difference is not significant, NNT is not meaningful.

Many meta-analysts use the natural logarithm of the OR, or *log odds ratio*, because it has better statistical properties. The log OR is distributed around 0 (instead of 1) and has an approximately normal distribution (standard deviation [SD] = 1.83). Positive values represent an increase in the odds; negative values represent a decrease in the odds. Log OR can be converted back to OR for ease of interpretation.

Effect Sizes for Continuous Data

Several ES metrics are available for continuous data. Here we describe ES for differences between groups, change over time (in one group), and correlations between two continuous variables.

Table 5.5. Point Estimates and Confidence Intervals for Dichotomous Data on Incarceration at One-Year Follow-Up (Ontario MST Trials)

Statistic	Point Estimate	95% Confidence Interval	
		Lower Bound	Upper Bound
Odds ratio	1.06	0.70	1.61
Risk ratio	1.04	0.79	1.38
Risk difference	0.01	−0.08	0.10

Group Contrasts

The *mean difference* is simply the average of the treatment group minus the average of the control group. In the Leschied and Cunningham (2002) study, youth in the MST group spent an average of 42.78 days in jail (SD = 117.98), compared with an average of 40.27 days (SD = 91.68) for youth in the control group. The mean difference is 42.78 minus 40.27, or 2.51 days (95% CI = −17.90 to 22.92). Since the CI spans the value of 0 (no difference between groups), the mean difference of 2.51 days is not statistically significant.

Using another example, Henggeler and colleagues (1999) randomly assigned 160 youth to MST or treatment as usual following referral for emergency psychiatric hospitalization. They reported a variety of outcome measures and included measures of family functioning based on the FACES Family Cohesion and Family Adaptability scales. Data on the first 113 cases show that MST cases had an average of 22.40 (SD = 6.85, N = 57) on the FACES Adaptability scale, compared with an average of 23.10 (SD = 6.20, N = 56) for control cases. The mean difference is −0.70 (95% CI = −3.11 to 1.71), a difference that is not statistically significant.

The mean difference is easy to interpret if readers are familiar with the scale. Thus, while the meaning of a difference in days (in the first example) is clear, a mean difference on the FACES Adaptability scale is not. Further, investigators report results of scales in a variety of ways. Some present raw data; others present standardized *z* scores.

The *standardized mean difference* (SMD) is useful when scores are reported in different ways or different scales are used to assess the same construct. The SMD, also known as *Cohen's d* (Cohen, 1969), is the mean difference divided by the pooled SD of the two groups. The pooled SD can be obtained from statistical software programs, from RevMan, and from a useful set of macros provided by David Wilson (mason.gmu.edu/~dwilsonb/ma.html). For the FACES Adaptability data presented above, the pooled SD is 6.536; the SMD = −0.70 divided by 6.536 = −0.107 (95% CI = −0.48 to 0.26). Since the SMD is expressed in SD units, this difference represents about one-tenth of an SD, a small effect. Further, the CI shows that the difference is not statistically significant.

To better illustrate the meaning of SMD, we show three hypothetical between-group comparisons in Figure 5.1. Adapted from Cooper (1998), the first distribution shows that there is no difference between the groups (SMD = 0). The second scenario shows a difference of 0.4. The third shows a difference of 0.85. Again, the difference (SMD) is expressed in terms of pooled SD units.

Glass (1976) proposed an ES metric for differences in averages that is slightly different from the SMD. In Glass's formula, the mean difference is divided by the SD of the control group. This is useful when treatment introduces additional variation in scores (Glass, McGaw, & Smith, 1981). When this occurs, the distribution of scores in the treatment group is wider (SD is larger) than in the control group. Glass's ES for the FACES Adaptability data is −0.70 divided by 6.20 = −0.113, slightly larger than the SMD.

Hedges (1981) showed that SMDs are upwardly biased when based on small samples (especially those with <20 participants), and he provided a simple correction for small-sample bias. Most meta-analysts use this correction, known as Hedges' $\hat{g}$, instead of SMD.

One-Group Pre–Post Contrasts

Studies that do not use control or comparison groups often report changes that occurred in one group between pretest (before treatment) and post-test (after treatment). When mean scores are available at two points in time, the difference between them (i.e., the post-test mean minus the pretest mean) is the *unstandardized mean gain score*. This score is divided by the pooled SD of the pretest and post-test scores to obtain a *standardized mean gain score*. Remember that these designs are vulnerable to many threats to internal validity, such as history, selection bias, maturation, and statistical regression (Shadish, Cook, & Campbell, 2002). Gain scores should never be combined (or confused) with SMDs: the former are derived from one group and the latter come from two groups.

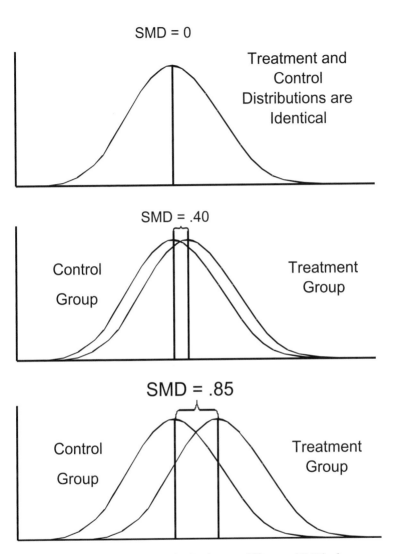

Figure 5.1. Understanding the standardized mean difference (SMD): three hypothetical situations. (Adapted from Cooper, 1998.)

Correlation Effect Size

The correlation coefficient r (formally called the *Pearson product-moment correlation coefficient*) expresses the strength and direction of an association between two continuous variables. It ranges from –1 to 1 and can be used as an ES metric. For purposes of meta-analysis, r is often converted to Fisher's Zr transformation, which has better statistical properties; Zr can be converted back to r.

Other Effect Size Metrics

Less common ES metrics include hazard rates for time-to-event data, ordinary least squares (OLS) regression coefficients, results of factor analysis, and data from receiver operating characteristics (ROC) curves. Meta-analytic techniques for most of these metrics are still under development.

Corrections for Error and Bias

We discussed selection bias and other within-study sources of bias in Chapter 4. In addition, there are at least two statistical sources of influence on the ES: small-sample bias and unreliable outcome measures.

As mentioned above, it is customary to use Hedges' $\hat{g}$ whenever small samples are included in meta-analysis, to compensate for small-sample bias. ESs from small samples can be unduly influenced by a single outlier. The presence of small-sample bias may be detected by examining the Forest plot closely or by creating funnel plots (discussed in Chapter 6).

When outcome measures are unreliable—due to sampling error, measurement error, low internal consistency, or range restrictions—the ES estimate may be biased. Range restrictions occur whenever distributions are artificially capped or constrained. For instance, income is often measured in ordinal categories, with one category that includes a very wide range of income levels at the high end (e.g., $100,000 and above). Income levels may be collapsed in various ways, depending on the population of interest. A study of middle-income families might restrict both the upper and lower levels to categories that have very wide ranges. Hunter and Schmidt (2004) have developed methods to correct for many sources of error and bias. Most of their work centers on the correlation ES.

Corrections for Clustering

Corrections are needed for unit of analysis errors when data from *cluster-randomized trials* (those that randomly assign groups, such as families or programs, to different conditions) have been analyzed at the individual level. As mentioned in Chapter 4, observations on individuals within clusters are not independent, yet unit of analysis errors are common in these kinds of trials. If clustering was accounted for in the original study, we can use the clustered (or cluster-adjusted) data in meta-analysis. If not, corrections are needed to produce accurate ES estimates.

To do this, we use the intraclass correlation coefficient (ICC) from the cluster-randomized trial or, if this is not available, the ICC from similar cluster-randomized studies. The ICC is a measure of the relative variation within and between clusters; it describes the similarity of results for individuals within clusters. Two methods for adjusting clustered data using the ICC are described here: the ICC is used to reduce each intervention group in the cluster-randomized trial to its "effective sample size" or to increase the standard errors of ES estimates.

In the first approach, the effective sample size is the original sample size divided by a "design effect." The design effect is $1 + (m - 1)r$, where m is the average cluster size and r is the ICC (Higgins & Green, 2006). Table 5.6 shows hypothetical results for four situations in which ICC is 0.02 or 0.05 and the average cluster size is 10 or 100. You can see that a larger ICC (which represents more similarity within clusters) produces a greater reduction in effective sample size. Larger clusters also produce greater design effects, reducing effective sample size. For dichotomous data, the design effect is applied to both the number of individuals who

Table 5.6. Two Methods Using the Intraclass Correlation Coefficient (ICC) to Correct for Clustering

Method 1: Adjust the Sample Size

ICC	Average Cluster Size (ACS)	Design Effect (DE)	Effective Sample Size (ESS)	ESS Rounded
0.02	10	1.18	8.47	8
0.05	10	1.45	6.90	7
0.02	100	2.98	33.56	34
0.05	100	5.95	16.81	17

Method 2: Adjust Standard Errors

Standard Error (SE) of Effect Size	DE	Square root of DE	Adjusted SE
0.1	1.18	1.09	0.11
0.1	1.45	1.20	0.12
0.1	2.98	1.73	0.17
0.1	5.95	2.44	0.24

$DE = 1 + (ACS - 1)^* ICC$; $ESS = ACS/DE$.

experienced the event and the total number in the intervention group. For continuous data, the design effect is applied to the sample size only (means and SDs are unchanged). Adjusted sample sizes are then rounded to the nearest whole number, which results in a loss of precision.

An alternative (and more flexible) approach is to multiply the SE of the effect estimate (ignoring clustering) by the square root of the design effect (Higgins & Green, 2006). The bottom portion of Table 5.6 presents hypothetical data for cases in which the standard error of ES is 0.1, and design effects are derived from the top portion of the table. We see that larger design effects produce greater increases in adjusted SEs. The adjusted SEs can be used in meta-analysis.

Once results of cluster-randomized trials have been adjusted for design effects they can be combined with other trials in meta-analysis, but reviewers should identify cluster-randomized trials as such and explain how they handled these data. Further, Higgins and Green (2006) recommend that reviewers use sensitivity analysis (described in Chapter 6) to see whether results are robust for inclusion of adjusted data from cluster-randomized trials, especially if ICCs are estimated from other studies.

Estimating Effect Sizes from a Variety of Data

Lipsey and Wilson (2001) show that SMDs can be calculated from a variety of statistics, including results of t-tests, F ratios from one-way ANOVA, and exact p values for t-tests. The SMD can be approximated from correlation coefficients and other statistics. The correlation coefficient can also be derived from a variety of statistics. Thus, when means and SDs are not available, meta-analysts can derive SMDs (or r's) from other information. Dichotomous outcomes can also be transformed into SMDs (Sanchez-Meca, Chacon-Moscoso, & Marin-Martinez, 2003), which is useful when outcomes are reported in different formats.

Interpretation of Effect Sizes

Cohen (1988) proposed the standards for interpreting OR, SMD, and r shown in Table 5.7. Lipsey and Wilson (2001) note that these standards are somewhat arbitrary; they discuss other interpretations of the magnitude of ES. Small effects may be meaningful in some contexts, such as when interventions are applied to large populations or target outcomes that are difficult to change.

It is often useful to express ES in metrics that are more familiar to practitioners and policy makers. For example, dichotomous data can

Table 5.7. Cohen's (1988) Standards for Interpreting Effect Size (ES)

ES Metric	Small Effect	Medium Effect	Large Effect
OR	1.5	2.5	4.3
SMD	0.2	0.5	0.8
R	0.1	0.25	0.4

OR: odds ratio; SMD: standardized mean difference; R: correlation coefficient.

easily be converted from risks to percentages. From the Leschied and Cunningham data on incarceration (see Table 5.4), we can say that 33% of youth in the MST group were incarcerated at 1 year, compared with 32% of those in the comparison group, an increase of 1% that is not statistically significant. Recall that Scher and colleagues (2006) used this approach to summarize data from 24 studies, which indicate that pregnancy occurred in 13.7% of the cases in treatment groups compared with 15% of comparison cases (see Fig. 1.1).

The interpretation of SMDs is not straightforward for readers who are unused to thinking about distributions of data in SD units. Similarly, correlation coefficients are not meaningful to many readers. For this reason, some analysts use the Rosenthal and Rubin (1983) binomial effect size display (BESD) to translate SMD or r into differences in "success" or "failure" rates. This makes use of the overlapping distributions of scores in the treatment and control groups (such as those shown in Figure 5.1) to express the concept of relative success or failure. For example, if SMD = 0, then half of the control cases and half of the treatment cases will have scores that fall about the mean. If SMD = 0.4, then 66% of treatment cases will have scores that are above the control group mean. This is equivalent to "success" rates of 40% in the control group and 60% in the treatment group, a 20% difference. If SMD = 0.85, 81% of the treatment cases will have scores above the control group mean; this is equal to a 30% success rate for control cases and a 69% success rate for the treatment group, a difference of 39%. This approach is explained in greater detail by Lipsey and Wilson (2001) and others.

Finally, it is important to note that the outcomes of interest, and corresponding ESs, may be positive or negative. For example, we tend to view some events (incarceration) as undesirable outcomes and other events (high school graduation) as desirable outcomes. Similarly, continuous measures are used to express desirable and undesirable outcomes (e.g., years of education, symptom severity). Some meta-analysts organize data so that positive values always reflect desirable outcomes, but that can lead to some confusion about what the outcome measure means. For instance, absence of incarceration is not as easily understood as an "event," even though it may be a desired outcome. Other meta-analysts report outcomes in their original form and make sure to explain the direction and meanings of effects.

Thus far we have discussed ESs that are calculated from individual studies. However, the purpose of meta-analysis is to use ES from multiple studies to better understand the distribution of effects and obtain better parameter estimates. Before we can do this, however, we must make sure that each ES is independent of all other ES estimates in the pool.

Avoiding Dependencies and Other Precautions

The calculation of a mean effect assumes that all of the study-level ESs are independent (Hedges, 1990). We must therefore avoid dependencies in meta-analysis. Dependencies occur when the study ESs included in a mean effect estimate are from overlapping samples.

Multiple Groups Within Studies

Multiple Treatments

When pooling data to create an overall mean, we must be sure that each study ES is independent of all other ESs in the same analysis. Each sample can contribute only one ES to an overall mean. If one study compares two different treatments with a single control group, it can produce two ESs (one for each treatment) using the same control group. However, we cannot include both estimates in the mean effect. Because they share the same control group, the cases in that control group would be "counted" twice, and the two estimates are not independent.

There are several options here:

- Select one ES estimate per study, either by selecting the treatment/ comparison contrast that is most relevant for our central question or by randomly selecting one treatment group (the decision should *not* be based on the size of the ES)

- Create separate mean effect estimates for different treatments
- Create an average of the study-level ES for use in calculating the mean effect

The last option would be defensible only if the differences between the treatment groups were not important for purposes of our meta-analysis. If a study compares a group that receives 6 weeks of treatment, another that receives 8 weeks, and a third that receives no treatment, the decision about whether to combine the 6- and 8-week treatments depends on how we have framed our central question. If length of treatment is a critical question, separate analysis may be useful. If not, the two treatment effects could be combined.

Different Counterfactual Conditions

Some studies compare one treatment with two different conditions, such as an alterative treatment and no treatment. Again, we must choose our comparisons carefully. One option is to select one comparison that is most relevant for our central question. If we are interested in relative effects, not absolute effects, we will choose the comparison group that received treatment, not the no-treatment group. Another option is to select the comparison condition that is most similar to those in other studies. A third choice is to analyze the comparisons separately. The latter is best if we want to assess both absolute effects (treatment compared to no treatment) and relative effects (compared with another treatment). Unless the two counterfactual conditions are very similar, information from two different control/comparison groups should not be combined (using averages or any other methods) in the same analysis.

Some studies compare a treatment group to a control group created by random assignment and a comparison group created by other means (for examples see Glazerman, Levy, & Myers, 2002). The comparison between groups created with random assignment is preferable because it supports more valid inferences about effects.

Subsamples

Some studies produce multiple estimates of ES that are truly independent. There may be one ES for girls and another for boys, or one ES for each of several sites. These can be included as separate ESs in the mean effect estimate, as long as there is no overlap between subsamples. Scher and colleagues (2006) did this in their meta-analysis of interventions to reduce teen pregnancy; they were able to obtain 34 independent estimates of effects on pregnancy risk from 24 studies because many studies reported separate effects for girls and boys. Separate ES estimates from multiple sites provide more detailed information on what happened where. Separate estimates can also increase the power to detect significant mean effects.

Multiple Measures of the Same Construct

Multiple measures of the same construct pose similar problems, because we cannot include multiple estimates from one sample in one overall effect estimate. We can do the following:

- Select one outcome measure on some basis (other than the size of the ES it produced)
- Create a study-level average across measures of the same construct for use in calculating a mean effect
- Create separate mean effect estimates for separate measures

We can select the most valid measure (e.g., biological tests over self-reported drug use). We can select the most commonly used measure to maximize comparability between studies. For instance, Corcoran and Pillai (2007) used the internalizing and externalizing scales from the Child Behavior Checklist in their meta-analysis of parent-involved treatment of child sexual abuse, since these scales were used in almost all the studies. They did not include other measures of internalizing symptoms (anxiety or depression) that were used in a few studies.

We could take an average of outcome measures of the same construct, for example combining different measures of internalizing behavior problems (taking care to calculate pooled standard deviations correctly). However, conceptually distinct outcomes and statistically unrelated outcomes should be kept separate in meta-analysis. If internalizing scores are not related to externalizing scores, combining them results in a loss of information on both measures.

Nugent (2006) argued that different measures should be linearly related if they are to be combined in the same mean effect estimate. His work relies on computer simulations, and it is not yet clear how closely those simulations resemble data on different measures from real samples. Conceptually, different measures of the *same* construct should be linearly related; if they are not, then it could be argued that they are measuring different constructs.

Multiple Reports on the Same Outcome Measure

Some studies gather information on a single outcome measure from different perspectives. Studies in the MST review assessed child behavior problems by obtaining reports on the Child Behavior Checklist (CBCL) from youth, parents, and teachers. They also assessed family functioning (using the FACES scales) from youth and parent perspectives.

One option is to analyze data from different reporters separately, as Corcoran and Dattalo (2006) did in their meta-analysis of parent-involved treatment of attention-deficit/hyperactivity disorder. Another option is to select one report for theoretical or practical reasons, as when one source is thought to be more important or valid than others. Bradley and Mandell's (2005) meta-analysis on interventions with child oppositional defiant disorder (ODD) relied on maternal reports only. The third option is to take an average of all the reports, triangulating data across sources. Pappadopulos and colleagues (Pappadopulos et al., 2006) took the latter approach, averaging results from multiple raters (clinicians, parents, and teachers) in their meta-analysis on medication for the treatment of child aggression. Littell, Popa, and Forsythe (2005) also used this approach in their MST review.

Averages will mask different viewpoints of reporters, so it is important to examine their concordance beforehand. To do this, we can examine correlations between different reports from different sources, if these are presented in a report or if we have access to the raw data. We can also perform sensitivity analysis (described in Chapter 6) to see if results vary across reporters; if not, there is some justification for combining these data.

Measures of Different Constructs

In the past, meta-analysts have created global estimates of effects by aggregating results across some or all outcome measures in a study. These study-level average ESs were then used in meta-analysis. In our view this is ill advised, because it conflates conceptually distinct outcome measures that may be statistically unrelated. For example, measures of out-of-home placement and child well-being may well be orthogonal (foster care may enhance well-being in some instances and have negative effects in others). A combined measure of placement/well-being obscures information on both outcomes. An intervention might have consistent effects on placement and mixed effects on well-being or vice versa. Important information for practice and policy will be lost if these outcomes are merged. Therefore, we think it best to keep conceptually distinct outcomes separate and perform multiple meta-analyses to estimate a mean ES for each relevant outcome.

The danger with multiple analyses is that they can inflate the overall Type I error—that is, as the number of statistical tests increases, so does the likelihood that some will turn out significant purely by chance. For this reason, it is important for the review team to decide in advance which outcomes are relevant for meta-analysis (see Chapter 2) and limit their analysis to these outcomes.

Multiple Follow-up Measures

Many studies provide repeated measures of outcomes using identical instruments and data sources. These outcomes are often assessed immediately after treatment and at one or more follow-up intervals. In general, immediate post-treatment assessments should be kept separate from follow-ups because they have different meanings; the first assesses immediate effects (and is more likely to be affected by expectancies), while the latter indicates whether effects last beyond treatment. Ideally, we will have several studies that measured outcomes at similar intervals. If so, we can compute separate mean effects for multiple points in time, which shows the durability of effects. However, studies rarely use identical intervals for outcome data collection. In this situation, we can create intervals for combining studies with similar follow-ups (e.g., 6 to 11 months, 12 to 24 months) or pick one point in time and use the study-level effect that is closest to this point. In the MST review, the authors used the ES estimate that was closest to a 1-year follow up for outcomes derived from administrative data and reported separate estimates for post-treatment and follow-up data derived from interviews. It is not wise to create a study-level average ES across all points in time, because information on the durability of effects is lost. ESs often deteriorate over time; hence it is important to present ES estimates within clear time frames.

Different ES Metrics

Different metrics should never be combined in the same meta-analysis. For example, a synthesis should not include both SMDs and standardized mean gain scores; these must be presented and synthesized separately.

Pooling Methods

One of the objectives of meta-analysis is to estimate an average effect across studies, and, although there are often more interesting analyses that can be performed, this is where most meta-analyses begin. Often the first question is, what is the average effect?

Mean effects can be calculated from two or more studies (Deeks et al., 2006). Some meta-analysts set a higher threshold, requiring more than two studies for the calculation of mean effects. However, we have not seen a convincing rationale for any arbitrary minimum greater than two. Statistical power analysis will show whether the studies in a meta-analysis are sufficient to detect significant overall effects and heterogeneity (Hedges & Pigott, 2001).

We begin our discussion of pooling methods by looking at data from multiple studies to see how they can be combined to produce mean effects. We use simple examples of dichotomous and continuous outcomes. Then, we take up issues of evaluating heterogeneity (or variation) among the study ESs. This leads us to a discussion of the choice between fixed effect and random effects models.

Mean Effects

The Leschied and Cunningham (2002) and Henggeler et al. (1999) studies mentioned above are two of eight RCTs included in the Cochrane and Campbell systematic review and meta-analysis of effects of MST (Littell, Popa, & Forsythe, 2005). Separate meta-analyses were performed for 21 conceptually distinct outcomes. Here, we arbitrarily selected the first and last outcomes reported in that review to use as examples; these outcomes are incarceration (a dichotomous variable) and FACES Adaptability scores (a continuous variable). The authors plotted data from all studies that reported data on each outcome of interest in Forest plots.

Table 5.8. Forest Plot for Incarceration (Dichotomous)

Study or Subcategory	Treatment n/N	Control n/N	OR (random) 95% Cl	Weight %	OR (random) 95% Cl
01 Leschied 2002	70/211	63/198		28.61	1.06 [0.70, 1.61]
02 Henggeler 1997	31/82	37/73		26.00	0.59 [0.31, 1.12]
03 Henggeler 1999a	19/58	16/60		24.00	1.34 [0.61, 2.96]
04 Henggeler 1992	9/43	28/41		21.39	0.12 [0.05, 0.33]
Total (95% Cl)	394	372		100.00	0.61 [0.27, 1.39]

Total events: 129 (Treatment), 144 (Control)
Test for heterogeneity: Chi^2 = 18.18, df = 3 (p = 0.0004), I^2 = 83.5%
Test for overall effect: Z = 1.18 (p = 0.24)

0.1 0.2 0.5   1   2   5   10
Favors treatment   Favors control

Source: Littell, Popa, & Forsythe, 2005.

The Forest plot for incarceration is shown in Table 5.8. Four RCTs provided data on the number or proportion of youth who were incarcerated at follow-up. The names of the studies are shown in the first column on the left. The meta-analysts ranked these studies according to their ability to support full intention to treat (ITT) analysis, which preserves the benefits of random assignment, within a standardized follow-up observation period. The Leschied and Cunningham study was the highest-ranked study in the group, so it appears at the top of the list, followed by other studies in rank order. The second and third columns from the left show the number of cases that experienced incarceration (n) and the total number of participants in the treatment and control groups (N). In the middle of the plot, the outcomes for each study are expressed as ORs, shown as squares, with 95% CIs that appear as lines extending from either side of the OR point estimate. The vertical line through the Forest plot is the "line of no effect" (OR = 1). Study effect sizes range from OR = 0.12 to OR = 1.34, but three of the four studies have confidence intervals that cross the line of no difference (i.e., they are not statistically significant). Only the lowest-ranked study shows a statistically significant effect. Another interesting feature of the OR distributions is that some studies produced results that tended to favor the treatment group, while others favored the control group.

Next we see the pooled (average) OR, which appears as a diamond in the center and below the study ORs. This pooled OR is an average of the four study ORs, but it is weighted using *inverse variance methods.* The inverse variance can be understood as a measure of precision; it is inversely related to the size of the CIs. Thus, studies with smaller CIs (greater precision) contribute more to the overall ES than those with wider CIs. Inverse variance methods take sample size and within-sample heterogeneity into account. (Larger samples and those with less heterogeneity produce more precise estimates.) The Leschied and Cunningham study has the smallest CIs and accounts for 28.9% of the overall estimate. The Henggeler 1992 study has the widest CIs and accounts for 21.4% of the overall estimate.

At the bottom of the Forest plot we see the legend, showing that results on the left of the center line (ORs < 1) favor treatment, while those to the right of the line (OR > 1) favor the control group. In other words, a reduction in incarceration in the treatment group is a favorable outcome.

The overall estimate represents the weighted average effect of MST on incarceration across these four studies, with a total of 766 participants. Here the estimate is OR = 0.61 with 95% CI = 0.27 to 1.39. When expressed as a risk ratio, the result is RR = 0.76, 95% CI = 0.48 to 1.22. Although this shows a trend toward a reduction in incarceration in the MST groups, the CI encompasses the value of 1, showing that the trend is not statistically significant. (Also, shown at the bottom left, the test for the overall effect Z is not significant, with $p = 0.24$.) We interpret this result with caution. This analysis provides no convincing evidence that MST reduces (or increases) incarceration, but this is *not the same as evidence of no effect*: the CI also encompasses ORs that have clinical and practical significance in both directions (a reduction in the risk of incarceration of 48% would be very meaningful, as would an increase of 22%). It is possible that when additional studies are added, the analysis will have enough statistical power to detect significant effects. Based on the present analysis, however, we conclude that there is no evidence of an effect.

Let us consider pooling of results on a continuous outcome measure before we take up some of the finer points of meta-analysis, such as heterogeneity and different estimation models. Table 5.9 shows a Forest plot with data from five RCTs that provided FACES Adaptability scores. As before, we ranked the studies on two aspects of quality (ITT analysis and standardized observation periods), but here we have two different subgroups of studies (one study supports ITT analysis and the other four do not), so we chose to look at these subgroups separately before we decide to create a pooled estimate across all five studies. The study with ITT analysis is followed by a diamond that shows results for this subgroup of one study. The SMD for this study is −0.11 (95% CI −0.48 to 0.62), a small, nonsignificant effect. Note that the "line of no difference" for SMD is set at 0.

Four studies compared FACES Adaptability scores for families who completed treatment (not all families in the MST group). Results are somewhat inconsistent across these studies and the overall (weighted)

104 Systematic Reviews and Meta-Analysis

Table 5.9. Forest Plot for FACES Adaptability Scores (Continuous)

Study or Subcategory	N	Treatment Mean (SD)	N	Control Mean (SD)	SMD (random) 95% CI	Weight %	SMD (random) 95% CI
03 ITT							
Henggeler 1999b	57	22.40 (6.85)	56	23.10 (6.20)	■	21.35	-0.11 [-0.48, 0.26]
Subtotal (95% CI)	57		56		◆	21.35	-0.11 [-0.48, 0.26]
Test for heterogeneity: not applicable							
Test for overall effect: Z = 0.56 (p = 0.57)							
05 TOT							
02 Henggeler 1997	75	29.00 (5.02)	65	29.75 (4.21)	■	23.32	-0.16 [-0.49, 0.17]
04 Henggeler 1992	33	-0.32 (1.79)	23	-0.67 (1.27)	■	14.29	0.22 [-0.32, 0.75]
Borduin 1995	70	0.13 (0.86)	56	-0.16 (0.71)	■	22.13	0.36 [-0.01, 0.72]
Ogden 2004	61	25.96 (3.95)	35	27.43 (4.80)	■	18.91	-0.34 [-0.76, 0.08]
Subtotal (95% CI)	239		179		◆	78.65	0.01 [-0.32, 0.34]
Test for heterogeneity: Chi² = 8.06, df = 3 (p = 0.04), I² = 62.8%							
Test for overall effect: Z = 0.08 (p = 0.94)							
Total (95% CI)	296		235		◆	100.00	-0.01 [-0.27, 0.24]
Test for heterogeneity: Chi² = 8.36, df = 4 (p = 0.08), I² = 52.1%							
Test for overall effect: Z = 0.10 (p = 0.92)							

```
        -1   -0.5    0    0.5    1
        Favors control   Favors treatment
```

Source: Littell, Popa, & Forsythe, 2005.

estimate for this subgroup is SMD = 0.01 (95% CI = −0.32 to 0.34), almost no effect. Thus, results from both subgroups are inconclusive, and the final pooled result shows little effect (SMD = −0.01, 95% CI = −0.27 to 0.24).

As you can see, the Forest plot is a useful way to display ES data from multiple studies. If we decide not to combine results, the Forest plot can be shown without a pooled estimate (overall mean). As mentioned above, many meta-analysts use log transformations before estimating mean ORs or SMDs. These techniques and many others are discussed by Lipsey & Wilson (2001) and by Deeks and colleagues (2006). Techniques for combining correlation effect sizes are described Hunter and Schmidt (2004).

Heterogeneity of Effect Sizes

Now that we have distributions of study ES on different outcome measures, we want to know how much variation there is within each of these distributions. Visual inspection of the funnel plots tells us something about the heterogeneity of results within and between studies. Are the differences between studies the result of sampling error (the heterogeneity we would expect to find among different samples drawn from the same population)? Or is there additional variance that cannot be accounted for by sampling error alone? Another way to frame this question is: Are all of our samples providing estimates of a single population effect, such that variation between them is purely due to chance? Or are there systematic differences between study ESs that may be due to variations in study, sample, or treatment characteristics?

There are several statistical tests for heterogeneity of ES. The Q statistic is a test for heterogeneity that has a χ^2 distribution (with $N-1$ degrees of freedom, where N is the number of ESs). Results of this test are reported at the bottom of Tables 5.8 and 5.9. In Table 5.8, this test ($\chi^2 = 18.18$, $df = 3$) is associated with a very small p value, which indicates the presence of significant heterogeneity (more than we would expect due to sampling error alone). Visual inspection of the Forest plots suggests that the heterogeneity evident in Table 5.8 may be due to an outlier, the last study in the plot. Although the χ^2 test in Table 5.9 is not statistically significant ($p = 0.08$), Deeks et al. (2006) caution that this test has low power when there are few studies in the meta-analysis.

Tables 5.8 and 5.9 also show another useful heterogeneity test, I^2. This is a measure of inconsistency that can be derived from the Q statistic (Higgins, Thompson, Deeks, & Altman, 2003). One of the advantages of this measure is that it does not depend on the number of studies in the meta-analysis. I^2 represents the percentage of the variation in effect estimates that is due to heterogeneity rather than sampling error (chance). A value greater than 50% can be considered substantial (Deeks et al., 2006). Both of our Forest plots show I^2 values that exceed 50%, so we conclude that there are substantial differences between studies on both outcome measures that are not explained by sampling error.

We have several options for handling heterogeneity in meta-analysis. One is to use random effects models, described below. If there are enough studies in the analysis, we can also use moderator analysis to explore possible sources of heterogeneity (this is discussed in Chapter 6). A third option is to show Forest plots without an estimate of the overall effect.

The decision to calculate an overall ES should be made in advance, based on the conceptual rationale developed earlier (see Chapter 2). At the outset, reviewers should have established a rationale for study inclusion criteria that explains what these studies have in common. At the protocol stage, the review team should have considered how to handle specific variations in treatments, samples, study designs, settings, and outcome measures. If there were good reasons to pool ES across studies then, analysts should follow that plan. It is illogical to plan an analysis of overall effects of an intervention and then make a post hoc decision that the studies were "too heterogeneous" to combine. If studies were "too heterogeneous" to combine in meta-analysis, why were they included in the review in the first place? Occasionally reviewers will encounter unanticipated issues that raise questions about the comparability of studies (perhaps the counterfactual conditions are entirely different); however, in the past, reviewers have been too quick to reject meta-analysis on the basis of heterogeneity. As we will see next, there are meta-analytic methods for studies that have heterogeneous effects.

Fixed Effect and Random Effects Models

Fixed effect and *random effects* models are the two main approaches for estimating mean effects. They are based on different assumptions about the nature of the studies and different definitions of combined effects. As a result, these models use different procedures to weight study ES, calculate mean effects, and produce CIs for mean effects (Bornstein, Hedges, & Rothstein, 2007).

Fixed effect (FE) models are based on the assumption that all of the studies come from the same population and produce estimates of one true ES. This assumes that "all factors which could influence the effect size are the same" in all studies (Bornstein et al., 2007, p. 22). The studies are viewed as "functionally equivalent," as when several studies of a drug are conducted by the same research team using the same dose and the same procedures in different cohorts (Bornstein et al., 2007). Between-study variation is expected to be due to sampling error alone and is ignored. Weights are assigned to studies based solely on within-study variance (using inverse variance methods, so that more precise study estimates receive greater weight).

Random effects (RE) models are based on the assumption that the true effect might vary across samples and studies. The effect might be larger or smaller, depending on the age, health, or wealth of participants, the length and intensity of treatment, study design artifacts, and so forth. In RE models, studies are assumed to be "a random sample of the relevant distribution of effects," and the combined effect estimates the mean of this distribution of true effects (Bornstein et al., 2007, p. 4). The mean effect in an RE model is influenced by variations between studies in addition to sampling error within studies. Weights are assigned to studies based on both sources of variance (the study inverse variance and a measure of between-study variance, called τ^2). Thus, compared with the FE model, the RE model takes more sources of variation into account. As a result, CIs for mean effects tend to be wider under the RE model than the FE model. However, if there is no significant heterogeneity, FE and RE models will produce similar results.

Large studies have more influence on the overall effect in FE models, since they provide more precise estimates of the one true effect. In contrast, the weights assigned to different studies are more balanced in RE models, because RE models are estimating a distribution of true effects, and each study may be estimating a different ES. One of the goals of the RE model is to produce results that generalize to a range of populations, while results of FE models generalize to a more narrowly defined population.

The choice between these models can (and usually should) be made in advance. Bornstein, Hedges, and Rothstein (2007) criticize an older practice of starting with FE models and then moving to RE models if there is statistical evidence of heterogeneity. They argue that it is better to choose the model that best reflects the underlying logic and assumptions of the analysis. Once we have specified the kinds of studies, populations, interventions, comparisons, and outcomes of interest, we should consider whether substantial heterogeneity is expected. If we believe that the studies in our meta-analysis will produce estimates of a single population ES, then the FE model is appropriate. If we include studies that vary in terms of their sample characteristics, interventions, and comparison conditions—and we think that some or all of these characteristics matter (i.e., influence effects)—then the assumptions of the FE model are untenable and the RE model is a better choice. This is often the case in meta-analyses of effects of psychosocial and health-care interventions. Thus, RE models were used in the MST review (see Tables 5.8 and 5.9).

Some reviewers claim that the studies they found were "too heterogeneous" to combine in a meta-analysis. This is not convincing, because RE models are well suited for meta-analysis with heterogeneous effects. Further, "when we decide to incorporate a group of studies in a meta-analysis we assume that the studies have enough in common that it makes sense to synthesize the information" from these studies (Bornstein et al., 2007, p. 11).

Conclusion

This chapter covered the meanings and measures of ES. We focused on common ES measures, especially the standardized mean difference (SMD) effect size, also known as Cohen's *d*. We noted that it is possible to convert most ES measures to SMDs. We discussed the importance of using confidence intervals (CIs) around estimated ESs to take into account variations due to sampling error and other sources. Forest plots show variations in effects within and between studies.

We considered ways to avoid dependencies in meta-analysis. This includes coping with multiple treatment or comparison groups, multiple measures and data sources, and data collected at multiple points in time.

We also described measures of heterogeneity and ways to handle heterogeneity of effects between studies. We explained the use of fixed effect (FE) and random effects (RE) models for estimating mean effects.

Main Points: Chapter 5

- An *effect size* is a measure of the strength (magnitude) and direction of a relationship between variables.
- ES metrics fall into three main categories: proportions, means, and correlations.
- Studies that test intervention effects and other kinds of causal inferences typically report differences (e.g., between pretests and post-tests, or between treated and untreated groups) in terms of proportions or average scores.
  - The *standardized mean difference* (SMD) is useful when mean scores are reported in different ways or different scales are used to assess the same construct.
  - The most commonly used ES measures for dichotomous data are the *odds ratio* (OR) and the *risk ratio* (RR). *Odds* refers to the chance that something will happen compared to the chance that it will not. *Risks* are probabilities.
- Studies that assess relationships between variables are likely to report measures of association (e.g., correlations).
- ESs are estimates and should be presented with *confidence intervals* that express the level of certainty (or precision) that accompanies the estimate.
- A decision to pool ESs across studies is made in advance, based on the conceptual model developed earlier.
- Prior to pooling ESs, analysts must make sure that each ES estimate has been adjusted for clustering (when data are from cluster-randomized trials) and is independent of all other ESs in the pool. Each sample can contribute only one ES estimate to a meta-analysis.
- Different ES metrics and conceptually distinct outcome measures should not be combined in the same meta-analysis.
- Reviews can produce separate meta-analyses (mean ES estimates and Forest plots) for conceptually distinct outcome measures.
- Mean effects are calculated by weighting each study ES according to its precision; inverse variance weights are used for this purpose.

- Forest plots are used to display study ES and confidence intervals, mean ES, and heterogeneity tests.
- The heterogeneity of effects across studies is examined to determine whether the variation is just due to chance (sampling error) or whether there are systematic differences due to study, sample, or treatment characteristics.
- Heterogeneity in meta-analysis can be handled by using Forest plots, random effects modeling, and moderator analysis.
- Fixed effect and random effects models are the two main approaches for estimating mean effects.
  - *Fixed effect* models assume that all studies come from the same population and produce estimates of one true ES.
  - *Random effects* models are based on the assumption that the true ES varies across samples and studies.

For Further Reading

Deeks, J. J., Higgins, J. T. P., & Altman, D. (Eds.) (2006). Analysing and presenting results. In J. P. T. Higgins & S. Green (Eds.), *Cochrane handbook for systematic reviews of interventions* 4.2.6; Section 8. In *The Cochrane Library, Issue 4, 2006.* Chichester, UK: John Wiley & Sons.

Lipsey, M. W., & Wilson, D. B. (2001). *Practical meta-analysis.* Thousand Oaks: SAGE.

6

Assessing Bias and Variations in Effects

In meta-analysis the most interesting questions often concern variations in effects. Are observed effects influenced by publication bias, study design, sample characteristics, intervention characteristics, and assessment of outcomes? Have effects been consistent over time? We begin this chapter with a discussion of ways to assess and adjust for publication bias, arguably the most potent source of bias in meta-analysis. Then we describe cumulative meta-analysis, a technique for assessing trends in the accumulation of evidence over time. Next we present methods for subgroup and moderator analysis, which explore variations in effect size (ES) for different groups created by methodological features and PICO (**p**opulations, **i**nterventions, **c**omparisons, and **o**utcomes) variables. We describe the use of meta-regression to estimate effects of one or more continuous moderators. Finally, we discuss ways to explore the consistency of results and the impact of various decisions that were made in the meta-analysis, using sensitivity analysis.

Publication Bias: Assessment and Adjustment

Publication bias is a potential threat to the internal validity of meta-analyses and should be considered carefully in the analysis and interpretation of results. Publication bias occurs when the results of published studies are not representative of results of all completed studies. As described in Chapter 1, publication bias is one of several sources of bias that affect the availability of primary studies for meta-analysis. Studies with positive, statistically significant results are published, cited, and reprinted more often than those with negative or null results (Dickersin, 2005).

Meta-analysts have developed several techniques to assess publication bias and adjust its influence in meta-analysis (Rothstein, Sutton, & Bornstein, 2005). These include the graphs and statistics described below.

One of the earliest techniques, the *failsafe N*, or file drawer number, was developed by Rosenthal (1979) and has been widely used. For meta-analyses with statistically significant overall mean effects, the failsafe *N* is the number of unpublished studies that would be required to change the results to a nonsignificant effect. Although the concept is attractive and easy to implement, Becker (2005) described several problems with this approach. There are several formulas for failsafe *N*, and they lead to widely varying estimates and different conclusions about whether publication bias is a threat to the results. Failsafe *N* does not take information on sample size or heterogeneity into account. It does not address questions about the magnitude of the effect. Further, there are no statistical criteria for interpreting failsafe *N*. Becker provides a convincing argument that "failsafe *N* should be abandoned in favor of other, more informative analyses" (2005, p. 124), such as those described below.

A simple graphical method for detecting publication bias and other sources of bias is the *funnel plot*. An example is shown in Figure 6.1. This technique is based on the assumption that, in the absence of significant heterogeneity, study ESs will be normally distributed around the mean effect. Smaller samples will produce less precise estimates (with wider

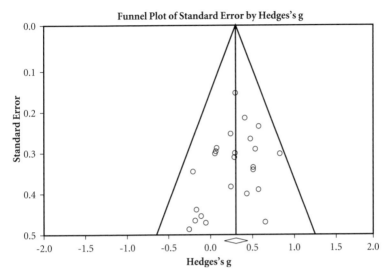

Figure 6.1. Funnel plot of standard error by effect size (Hedges' $\hat{g}$) for overall reading scores. *Source*: Ritter, Denny, Albin, Barnett, & Blankenship, 2006.

confidence intervals [CIs]), so the distribution of ESs from small samples will be wider than the distribution of ESs from large samples. If we plot the results of each study in the meta-analysis with ES on the x-axis and sample size or a measure of the precision of the ES estimate (usually the standard error) on the y-axis, the result should resemble an inverted funnel (Light & Pillemer, 1984). The distribution of ESs should be small at the top of the plot (where larger and more precise studies are shown) and wider at the bottom.

In the absence of publication bias, the distribution of ESs will be symmetrical. Publication bias will produce asymmetry within the funnel, because studies with statistically significant effects in the desired direction will be available and those with null and contradictory results will be missing. The ESs will cluster on one side of the funnel.

Publication bias is not the only source of asymmetry in funnel plots, however (Egger et al., 1997b). Small studies may produce larger ESs when their design and analytic methods are less rigorous or when treatment is implemented with greater care than in larger studies. Thus, the funnel plot is a generic tool to examine the tendency for smaller studies to show larger treatment effects (Sterne, Becker, & Egger, 2005).

The funnel plot in Figure 6.1 shows results for overall reading scores from 24 studies of effects of volunteer tutoring programs (Ritter et al., 2006). Visual inspection of the funnel plot shows no evidence of asymmetry, possibly because the meta-analysis included results from 13 unpublished dissertations.

Visual inspection of funnel plots is subjective and should be balanced with additional analyses. There are several statistical tests for asymmetry. These should be thought of as tests for "small-sample bias." Since the statistical power of these tests is low, they should be used only when there are at least 10 studies in the meta-analysis (and at least one has statistically significant results). Asymmetry tests are somewhat controversial and can produce inconsistent results (Ioannidis & Trikalinos, 2007).

Duvall and Tweedie developed the trim-and-fill method to assess and adjust for publication bias and small-sample bias (Duval, 2005). This method uses an iterative process in which unmatched observations are removed from the funnel plot (trimming the distribution) and then imputed values for missing studies are added, filling in estimates of the ES and standard errors of studies that are likely to be missing. The appearance of many missing studies on one side of the line of mean effect is suggestive of publication bias or small-sample bias. Ritter and colleagues (2006) used the trim-and-fill method for the plot in Figure 6.1 and found no evidence of publication or small-sample bias.

Results of another trim-and-fill analysis, shown in Figure 6.2, are from Smedslund and colleagues' (2006) meta-analysis of work programs for welfare recipients. Available studies produced a small, positive mean effect for employment status; this is represented by the open diamond below the bottom axis. Trim-and-fill analysis suggested that more than a dozen studies might be missing. After imputing missing data, authors obtained an adjusted mean effect represented by the black diamond below the x-axis. A comparison of the observed mean effect with the trim-and-fill adjusted mean effect suggests that the observed effect may be overestimated. Publication bias is one of several possible

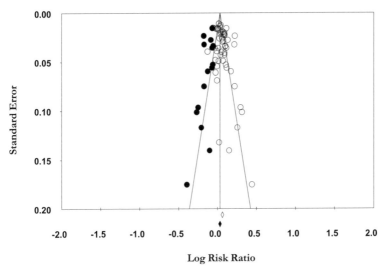

Figure 6.2. Funnel plot of standard error by log risk ratio for employment status. Open circles signify the actual studies. Closed circles are virtual imputed studies that would be expected if there were no publication bias present in the data. *Source*: Smedslund et al., 2006.

explanations, but only 11 of the 102 citations included in the meta-analysis were published in journals (Smedslund et al., 2006). Small-sample effects do not account for asymmetry in this case, because some of the "missing" studies appear at the top of the funnel. There are other sources of "availability" bias (including outcome reporting and dissemination bias) that might account for asymmetry. Smedslund and colleagues found evidence of bias (asymmetry) for three of their four outcome measures.

Objections to the trim-and-fill method include discomfort with imputation of data from "fictional" studies. This objection must be balanced against concerns about the systematic omission of real studies that are not readily available precisely because of the direction of their results. Therefore, Duval (2005) recommends that reviewers use trim-and-fill as a form of sensitivity analysis (discussed further on) to see whether results are robust for publication bias and related biases.

When study effects are heterogeneous, more complex weight function models are better suited to analysis of publication bias (Hedges & Vevea, 2005).

Suggestions for preventing outcome reporting, publication, and dissemination biases are well developed. Aside from the need for extensive searches for gray literature, these proposals—which center on the need for routine, prospective registration of studies—are beyond the scope of this book. (Interested readers should see Rothstein, Sutton, & Bornstein, 2005.)

Cumulative Meta-Analysis

Cumulative meta-analysis is a method of tracking trends in research on a given topic over time (or some other function). The simplest way to do this is with a Forest plot in which study effects are sorted by year of publication (or report date for unpublished studies). Combined effects can be calculated cumulatively to show what conclusions could be drawn from the body of research over time. As new studies are added, the average effect size may increase, decrease, fluctuate, or remain stable. Initial studies may produce disparate results that converge over time (Ioannidis & Lau, 2001). Initially positive effects may deteriorate over time when early results are not replicated in different situations or by different investigators (Trikalinos et al., 2004). However, when effects are stable over a series of studies, at a certain point the combined effect may be well established and statistically significant. For example, Gilbody and colleagues (Gilbody et al., 2006) showed that by the year 2000 there was sufficient evidence of the superiority of collaborative care over routine primary care for depression.

Bornstein (2005) demonstrated the use of cumulative meta-analysis to assess publication bias or small-sample effects. Instead of sorting by year, studies are sorted by their precision (from most to least precise) in a Forest plot or cumulative Forest plot. If the gradual inclusion of studies with lower precision increases the mean effect estimate, there is evidence of publication bias or a small-study effect.

Subgroup and Moderator Analysis

Treatment effects (and relationships between variables, more generally) are often inconsistent across populations, intervention types, comparison conditions, and outcome measures. Methodological features also account for substantial variations in ES across studies (Wilson & Lipsey, 2001). In planning a meta-analysis, we often have hypotheses about variables that may moderate effects. These hypotheses should be explicit in the protocol for a systematic review, and serve as a guide for subgroup and moderator analysis.

Subgroup Analysis

There may be good reasons to estimate effects for certain groups that are subsets of our population of interest. In their review of pregnancy prevention programs, Scher and colleagues (2006) estimated separate effects of different types of programs for middleschool youth, high school youth, and mixed-age groups. The analysis shown in Table 6.1 shows that different programs tend to target different age groups, but most effects are small, and none reduces risks by more than 15% (for ease of interpretation, authors converted risk differences to percentages; $RD < 0.15$). The tests of significance indicate whether effects were significant within subgroups, not whether age or intervention type was associated with systematic variations in effect size. Thus it is a descriptive analysis, not a moderator analysis (the authors did perform moderator analysis, which will be described below).

Subgroup analyses should be limited in number and planned in advance. As the number of subgroup analyses increases, so does the likelihood that statistically significant results will be found in at least one subgroup due to chance alone (Type I error). These results tend to be misinterpreted, especially if overall results are not significant. There is a temptation to conclude that the intervention worked in some groups, when overall effects are not significant.

Results of subgroup analysis are commonly misrepresented as tests of differential effects. It is not appropriate to compare results across

Table 6.1. Pooled Estimates of the Percentage Point Impacts of Programs on Sexual Experience, Pregnancy Risk, and Pregnancy, by Grade Levels of Youth Targeted

Type of Program and Outcome	Middle School		High School		Mixed Grade Levels	
	# of impact estimates	Estimated impact	# of impact estimates	Estimated impact	# of impact estimates	Estimated impact
All interventions						
Sexual experience	24	−0.8%	7	−0.9%	9	−3.8% **
Pregnancy risk	16	0.1%	8	−11.1% ***	10	−4.0%
Pregnancy	13	0.3%	8	−2.7%	4	−5.6%
One-time consultations						
Sexual experience	0	n.a.	1	n.a.	0	n.a.
Pregnancy risk	1	n.a.	3	−7.6%	0	n.a.
Pregnancy	1	n.a.	0	n.a.	0	n.a.
Sex education with abstinence focus						
Sexual experience	9	1.0%	0	n.a.	0	n.a.
Pregnancy risk	5	0.5%	0	n.a.	0	n.a.
Pregnancy	7	1.0% *	0	n.a.	0	n.a.

Sex education with contraception component

Sexual experience	12	−1.7%	1	n.a.	4	−2.0%
Pregnancy risk	10	−0.2%	4	−14.6%	5	−3.7%
Pregnancy	2	−0.6%	3	−2.5%	0	n.a.

Multi-component/youth development programs

Sexual experience	3	−9.2%	5	0.0%	5	−5.8% **
Pregnancy risk	0	n.a.	1	n.a.	5	−4.8%
Pregnancy	3	−5.1%	5	−2.5%	4	−5.6% *

Note: Estimates are based on random-effects models estimated using comprehensive meta-analysis (Bornstein & Rothman, 1999).

n.a.: not applicable due to either no studies or only one study in this category.

*** $p < 0.01$; ** $p < 0.05$; * $p < 0.10$.

Source: Scher et al., 2006.

subgroups without performing moderator analysis; that is, we need to test whether results are statistically different for subgroups. It may be tempting to conclude (on the basis of the data in Table 6.1) that interventions are more effective in reducing pregnancy risk among high school students compared with middle school students. However, that comparison has not been tested here. Further, we don't see the CIs for effects within subgroups and cannot judge their overlap.

Moderator Analysis

Moderator analysis provides directs tests of the differences between subgroups and influences of variables (moderators) on the mean effect. Scher and colleagues (2006) found that programs with a contraceptive focus achieved significantly greater reductions in pregnancy risk among high school youth compared with middle school students, although the effects were not statistically significant in either of these subgroups.

As with subgroup analysis, moderator analysis should be planned in advance and limited to central questions in the meta-analysis. Moderator analysis can be used to explore possible sources of heterogeneity in combined effects. It is generally used to pursue important theoretical or practical questions—and this can be done regardless of whether there is substantial heterogeneity in the Forest plots.

There are two main methods for moderator analysis. One uses an analog to the analysis of variance (ANOVA); the other uses a version of multiple regression. (Note that these methods are not the same as ordinary ANOVA and OLS regression, and those routines should never be applied to meta-analytic data.) Both approaches require at least 10 studies for every moderator in the analysis (Higgins & Green, 2006).

A final caveat before we turn to examine moderator analysis more closely: moderator analysis is essentially an observational (nonexperimental) inquiry. Studies are not randomly assigned to moderators. Moderator analysis does not support causal inferences; rather, it generates hypotheses about *potential* sources of heterogeneity and differential effects.

Analog to the Analysis of Variance

In the ANOVA analog, the moderator is a categorical variable. Average ESs are calculated for each category, and tests of significance are used to assess differences between groups. One can use this approach to see, for example, whether effects produced by randomized experiments differ from those produced by nonrandomized studies, whether treatment effects differ in samples of younger versus older children, or whether there are different effects for short-term versus long-term treatment.

Using the ANOVA analog, Scher and colleagues (2006) assessed the durability of program impacts on three outcomes (Table 6.2). They found greater effects at the short-term follow-up (less than 1 year after intervention) than in later follow-ups, but the trend was significant for only one of three outcome variables.

Smedslund assessed the potential impact of design quality moderators on program effects on employment. Table 6.3 shows the risk ratios and confidence intervals for effects within different categorical ratings on design quality variables. Heterogeneity within groups is evaluated with the Qw statistic and I^2. There is substantial heterogeneity within most categories. The Q statistic shows the variance between categories (Qb), which is statistically significant for two design quality moderators and not significant for four design moderators.

Table 6.4 shows results of similar analyses of associations between program characteristics and employment outcomes (for results of additional moderator analyses, see Smedslund et al., 2006). Again, effects are heterogeneous within most categories. Results suggest that programs focusing on employment had greater effects on employment than those targeting education. Programs providing assistance with a job search had greater impacts than those that did not. There were no differences by level of enforcement, provision of work experience, education, time limits, financial assistance, skills training, or child care. Studies conducted by MDRC tended to produce greater effects than those run by other evaluators. Although it is tempting to overinterpret results of moderator analysis, we should not conclude that a focus on employment and job search assistance produce greater effects than other

Table 6.2. Pooled Estimates of the Impacts of Programs on Sexual Experience, Pregnancy Risk, and Pregnancy, by Duration of Follow-up Characteristics

	Sexual Experience			Pregnancy Risk			Pregnancy		
	# of impact estimates	Estimated impact[a]	p-value	# of impact estimates	Estimated impact[a]	p-value	# of impact estimates	Estimated impact[a]	p-value
All interventions	40	−1.2%	0.113	34	−1.3%	0.115	25	−0.4%	0.443
Duration of follow-up								***	
Less than one year	6	−4.2%	0.144	6	−5.9%	0.106	3	−6.9%	0.000
One year to twenty-three months	17	−0.4%	0.636	16	−2.6%	0.043	10	0.6%	0.058
Two years or more	17	−1.3%	0.276	12	−0.3%	0.721	12	−1.8%	0.121

Note: Estimates are based on random-effects models estimated using comprehensive meta-analysis (Bornstein & Rothman, 1999).
n.a. means not applicable.
*** $p < 0.01$; ** $p < 0.05$; * $p < 0.10$.
Source: Scher et al, 2006.

Table 6.3. Effects of Design Quality Moderators on Employment

Moderator	k	Risk Ratio	Lower Limit	Upper Limit	k	Q_w (df)	I^2	Q_B (df)	p_B
Random allocation*									
Met	12	1.064	1.016	1.115	0.008	53.9 (11)	79.6	26.0 (3)	0.000
Unclear	48	1.070	1.049	1.092	0.000	336.4 (47)	86.0		
Not met	2	1.031	0.890	1.194	0.686	16.0 (1)	93.8		
Allocation concealment									
Met	15	1.073	1.031	1.118	0.001	82.0 (14)	82.9	2.798 (2)	0.247
Unclear	47	1.066	1.045	1.089	0.000	347.4 (46)	86.8		
Performance bias*									
Met	23	1.055	1.018	1.094	0.003	144.9 (22)	84.8	7.93 (3)	0.047
Unclear	30	1.057	1.035	1.080	0.000	168.0 (29)	82.7		
Not met	9	1.119	1.056	1.187	0.000	73.3 (8)	89.1		
Detection bias									
Met	57	1.067	1.047	1.088	0.000	421.2 (56)	86.7	0.559 (1)	0.454
Unclear	6	1.049	1.006	1.093	0.025	8.8 (5)	43.5		

(continued)

Table 6.3. (continued)

Moderator	k	Risk Ratio	Lower Limit	Upper Limit	k	Q_w (df)	I^2	Q_B (df)	p_B
Attrition bias									
Met	38	1.072	1.050	1.095	0.000	253.3 (37)	85.4	0.817 (2)	0.665
Unclear	16	1.064	1.024	1.106	0.001	117.1 (15)	87.2		
Not met	9	1.041	0.979	1.108	0.202	37.5 (8)	78.7		
Intention to treat									
Met	30	1.077	1.052	1.104	0.000	207.7 (29)	86.0	1.955 (2)	0.376
Unclear	31	1.055	1.028	1.082	0.000	169.8 (30)	82.3		
Not met	2	1.493	0.606	3.677	0.384	25.3 (1)	96.0		

* Statistically significant difference.
Source: Smedslund et al., 2006.

Table 6.4. Effects of Categorical Moderators on Employment

Moderator	k	Risk Ratio	Lower Limit	Upper Limit	k	Q_w (df)	I^2	Q_B (df)	p_B
*Focus of intervention**									
Employment	41	1.087	1.056	1.119	0.000	311.7 (40)	87.2	8.630 (3)	0.035
Education	12	1.048	1.024	1.073	0.000	40.5 (11)	72.9		
Other	8	1.026	0.990	1.062	0.156	45.7 (7)	84.7		
Unclear	2	1.032	1.001	1.063	0.042	0.5 (1)	0.0		
Enforcement									
Mandatory	48	1.061	1.042	1.080	0.000	324.1 (47)	85.5	1.816 (1)	0.178
Voluntary	15	1.116	1.039	1.199	0.003	101.3 (14)	86.2		
Work experience									
Yes	50	1.072	1.052	1.093	0.000	333.1 (49)	85.3	2.69 (2)	0.260
No	12	1.047	0.992	1.105	0.094	91.9 (11)	88.0		
Education									
Yes	29	1.067	1.039	1.095	0.000	253.0 (28)	88.9	0.0 (1)	1.000
No	34	1.067	1.041	1.093	0.000	174.6 (33)	81.1		
Time limits									
Yes	11	1.074	1.013	1.138	0.017	110.7 (10)	91.0	0.066 (1)	0.798
No	52	1.065	1.046	1.085	0.000	316.8 (51)	83.9		

(continued)

Table 6.4. (continued)

Moderator	k	Risk Ratio	Lower Limit	Upper Limit	k	Q_w (df)	I^2	Q_B (df)	p_B
Financial incentives									
Yes	18	1.072	1.026	1.121	0.002	140.4 (17)	87.9	0.080 (1)	0.777
No	45	1.065	1.044	1.086	0.000	290.7 (44)	84.9		
Job search*									
Yes	38	1.087	1.064	1.111	0.000	231.9 (37)	84.0	8.628 (1)	0.003
No	25	1.031	1.003	1.060	0.028	147.4 (24)	83.7		
Skills training									
Yes	24	1.056	1.029	1.083	0.000	148.2 (23)	84.5	0.678 (1)	0.410
No	39	1.071	1.046	1.098	0.000	266.1 (38)	85.7		
Child care									
Yes	17	1.087	1.047	1.129	0.000	83.3 (16)	80.8	1.471 (1)	0.225
No	46	1.059	1.038	1.080	0.000	325.2 (45)	86.2		
Evaluator*									
MDRC	37	1.092	1.070	1.116	0.000	228.9 (36)	84.3	14.786 (4)	0.005
Mathematica	6	1.033	0.979	1.091	0.024	17.0 (5)	70.6		
Abt Associates	7	1.018	0.976	1.061	0.405	21.6 (6)	72.2		
University	9	1.021	0.969	1.076	0.428	59.1 (8)	86.5		
Other	4	1.013	0.923	1.112	0.783	9.5 (3)	68.3		

* Statistically significant difference. *Source:* Smedslund et al., 2006.

strategies. Again, these are nonexperimental comparisons and the associations may be spurious; other factors associated with these moderators may be responsible for observed differences between subgroups.

Meta-Regression

Meta-regression is used to assess the potential impact of one or more continuous or categorical moderators. Similar to multiple regression analysis, meta-regression has one dependent variable and a set of continuous independent variables. Here the dependent variable is an ES, the independent variables are moderators, and the unit of analysis is the study. Meta-regression can be performed under the fixed effect or random effects models. As mentioned above, this should not be attempted unless there are at least 10 studies for each moderator in the analysis (Higgins & Green, 2006).

Assumptions of multiple regression analysis are applicable to meta-regression. Categorical variables can be expressed as a set of dummy variables with one omitted category. Since moderators may be confounded, analysts should examine a correlation matrix before developing meta-regression models. As with OLS regression, there are techniques for assessing violations of assumption, including normal distributions (heteroskedasticity, linearity, and absence of multicolinearity). To that end, a scatter plot of the independent and dependent variables can easily be produced by most meta-analysis programs.

Smedslund et al. (2006) conducted meta-regression to assess potential impacts of continuous moderators on ES. They first presented a correlation matrix that included all of the moderators in the analysis. Table 6.5 shows results of the meta-regression. Mean age was associated with greater likelihood of employment. Programs with higher proportions of Caucasians and/or persons of African decent tended to have lower employment rates than other programs. Sanctions were associated with lower employment, while regional unemployment rates predicted higher levels of employment among program participants. Again, the Q χ^2 test shows that there is substantial heterogeneity of effects within these categories.

Table 6.5. Effects of Continuous Moderators on Employment (Meta-Regression)

Moderator	Slope	SE Slope	Lower Limit	Upper Limit	Residual Q	df	p Value
Collection start	−0.00135	0.00095	−0.00321	0.00051	377.5	52	0.00000
Mean age	0.00829*	0.00156	0.00525	0.01134	302.4	52	0.00000
Percent males	−0.00025	0.00022	−0.00068	0.00019	428.9	59	0.00000
Percent Whites	−0.00033*	0.00016	−0.00063	−0.00003	370.4	58	0.00000
Percent Blacks	−0.00029*	0.00014	−0.00056	−0.00002	385.8	59	0.00000
Percent Hispanics	0.00026	0.00017	−0.00008	0.00059	320.9	48	0.00000
Percent with GED or high school diploma	−0.00008	0.00017	−0.00042	0.00025	350.6	56	0.00000
Duration of intervention	0.00099	0.00036	0.00029	0.00170	407.3	58	0.00000
Percent sanctioned	−0.00203*	0.00038	−0.00277	−0.00129	203.9	34	0.00000
Regional unemployment	0.00915*	0.00160	0.00601	0.01229	358.1	60	0.00000
Number of intervention elements	0.00625	0.00319	0.00000	0.01250	428.4	61	0.00000

* 95% confidence interval for the regression slope does not cross zero; the moderator has a statistically significant effect for that outcome. SE: standard error. *Source*: Smedslund et al., 2006.

One of the main limitations of meta-regression is that it requires a fairly large number of studies. Statistical power is affected by the number of studies and number of moderators in the analysis. Perhaps the most important limitation is that one cannot draw causal conclusions from meta-regression.

Sensitivity Analysis

Sensitivity analysis is not the same as subgroup analysis. The latter is used to assess effects for distinct subsamples (e.g., for boys versus girls) and, when combined with moderator analysis, to see whether interventions might have differential effects for different subgroups. Sensitivity analysis refers to assessments of decisions made during the review process.

Many decisions are made throughout the review process and meta-analysis. In general, the purpose of sensitivity analysis is to determine whether results are robust (consistent) under different assumptions, and to test the impact of decisions that have been made during the review process (Egger et al., 1997a). This involves comparing two or more models. For example, one study might produce an extreme ES, raising questions about whether it belongs in the distribution of study ES or is unduly affected by error. Pooled ES can be calculated with and without this outlier to see whether results are sensitive to (changed by) the inclusion or exclusion of this study.

Sensitivity analysis can be used to determine whether results would be affected by shifts in the study inclusion/exclusion criteria (by design features or other study characteristics). In a review of Scared Straight programs, authors examined the impact of including in the meta-analysis studies that were deficient in one or more design quality (inadequate random assignment, high attrition, or absence of blinding) or fidelity criteria (Petrosino, Turpin-Petrosino, & Buehler, 2003). Authors dropped each study that was deficient in some respect and then re-calculated the mean effect to examine the impact of this study on the overall results.

Sensitivity analysis is also used to explore the potential impact of missing data on overall results. When studies provide sufficient information to calculate ES for some outcomes and not others, it is possible that the missing data are not random. In fact, null results are more likely to be missing or underreported (Chan et al., 2004). Meta-analysts handle this in several ways, often imputing different values for missing data (assuming missing ESs are equal to zero, equal to the average ES, etc.) and testing results. Smedslund and colleagues (2006) used sensitivity analysis to determine whether results were robust across different methods of handling missing data. For results that were reported as nonsignificant, investigators estimated ESs and their standard errors using three different assumptions: p value $= 0.1$, 0.55, and 0.99. Each assumption was then employed in calculating pooled ESs. Sensitivity analyses were also used for meta-regression by comparing results for one analysis that excluded studies with missing data with another that included imputed means for missing data (Smedslund et al., 2006).

As mentioned above, the trim-and-fill method can be considered a form of sensitivity analysis. It explores the possibility that the sample of studies is biased toward larger studies and those with positive results. Trim-and-fill-adjusted ES estimates are compared with observed ESs to see whether the latter are robust for publication and small-sample biases.

Statistical Power

Hedges and Pigott (2001) developed methods for assessing the statistical power of several tests that are commonly used in meta-analysis, including the ability to determine whether a combined ES is significantly different from zero, and the power of heterogeneity tests and moderator analysis. Power analysis can be used a priori, to decide what kinds of analyses will be performed, or in post hoc assessments. The latter may be useful when overall ESs are not statistically significant, since inadequate statistical power is a possible explanation for null results. Indeed, in the MST review, post hoc analysis showed that there was insufficient power (likely due to the small number of studies in the analysis) to determine whether effects were significantly different from zero (Littell, Popa, & Forsythe, 2005).

Conclusion

In this chapter, we have discussed ways to detect publication bias and assess its influence, describing the methods that have been most recently advanced. Other major topics of discussion in this chapter were subgroup and moderator analysis, including meta-regression, to explore variations in ESs due to methodological features and PICO (populations, interventions, comparisons, and outcomes) variables in the primary studies. Sensitivity analysis has been used to discover the extent to which results of meta-analysis are robust for outliers and for decisions and assumptions made during the analysis. Finally, statistical power analysis is an important tool for planning and evaluating meta-analyses.

Main Points: Chapter 6

- Some assessment of *publication bias* should be included in any meta-analysis. Reviewers should not use the *failsafe N*. The *funnel plot* is a simple graphical method for detecting associations between study precision and effect size. In the absence of significant heterogeneity, *trim-and-fill analysis* should be used to investigate the potential impact of publication bias on conclusions.
- *Cumulative meta-analysis* is a method of tracking trends in research over time (or by another continuous factor).
- *Subgroup analysis* estimates effects for certain groups that are subsets of the population of interest.
- *Moderator analysis* provides more direct tests of the differences between subgroups and influences of variables (moderators) on the mean effect and includes two methods: an analog to the analysis of variance (ANOVA) (when the moderator is a

categorical variable) and *meta-regression*, a version of multiple regression that is used when there are one or more continuous moderators.

- *Sensitivity analysis* is used to determine whether results are consistent under different assumptions, to test the impact of decisions that have been made during the review process, and to explore the potential impact of missing data on overall results.
- *Statistical power analysis* is useful in planning and interpreting meta-analyses.

For Further Reading

Cooper, H., Hedges, L. V., & Valentine, J. (in press). *Handbook of research synthesis* (2nd ed.). New York: Russell Sage Foundation.

Higgins, J. P. T., & Green, S. (Eds.). (2006). *Cochrane handbook for systematic reviews of interventions.* Chichester, UK: John Wiley & Sons.

Lipsey, M. W., & Wilson, D. B. (2001). *Practical meta-analysis.* Thousand Oaks: SAGE Publications.

Petticrew, M., & Roberts, H. (2006). *Systematic reviews in the social sciences: A practical guide.* Oxford, UK: Blackwell Publishing.

Rothstein, H., Sutton, A. J., & Bornstein, M. (Eds.). (2005). *Publication bias in meta-analysis: Prevention, assessment, and adjustments.* Chichester, UK: Wiley.

Sutton, A. J., Abrams, K. R., Jones, D. R., Sheldon, T., & Song, F. (2000). *Methods for meta-analysis in medical research.* Chichester, UK: Wiley.

7

Conclusions

This chapter considers the kinds of conclusions that can be drawn from systematic reviews with or without meta-analysis. We describe common mistakes in interpretation and ways to avoid them. Finally, we reflect on the current status and likely future of the science of research synthesis, and the implications of this science for social work.

Interpreting and Summarizing Results

Great care goes into the conduct of a good systematic review; this should be matched with careful use of language in the interpretation and summary of results. Summaries that are both accurate and accessible (nontechnical) will maximize the utility of a review. Such summaries are not easy to write, however. Many examples of good, plain-language summaries of systematic reviews and meta-analyses can be found in the Cochrane Database of Systematic Reviews. Typically, these summaries are not written by review authors but by individuals who represent likely end users of the review (policy makers, practitioners, or consumers). The summaries are then vetted and approved by the review authors.

Reviewers often present preliminary results for discussion at conferences and in meetings with policy makers and practitioners. This is an excellent way to develop accessible presentations and obtain input on interpretations and summaries of results. Users groups and advisory boards can be very helpful in this regard.

Results of Meta-Analysis

Generally reviewers describe results of meta-analysis in terms of the direction and size of the point estimates (mean effects), the width and position of their confidence intervals (CIs), heterogeneity (consistency) of effects, and the strength (quality) of evidence, including any concerns about potential publication bias. It is tempting to begin a summary by describing the point estimates and CIs. Indeed, many observers think the "bottom line" in a meta-analysis is represented by the diamonds at the bottom of our Forest plots. However, it is more prudent to begin with a discussion of the quality of available evidence and the potential for bias, and then describe the heterogeneity of effects across studies, and the CIs around mean effects. This is because the direction and size of mean effects is not particularly meaningful if the quality of evidence is weak, heterogeneity is large, and/or CIs cross the line of no effect.

Quality of Evidence

Reviewers can describe the quality of a body evidence in light of their judgments of the qualities (design features) and risk of bias in the primary studies (see Chapter 4) and of the likelihood of publication and related biases in the sample of studies as a whole (Chapter 6). The GRADE system for assessing the quality of evidence (GRADE Working Group, 2004) has been used in some Cochrane and Campbell reviews (e.g., Smedslund et al., 2006). Using this system, reviewers rate the quality of evidence for each outcome measure in terms of the strength of research designs, consistency of results, and other considerations. GRADE does not explicitly incorporate judgments about publication or small-sample bias.

Heterogeneity of Results

The statistical heterogeneity of main effects is assessed in terms of the significance of Q (χ^2 test) and the size of I^2 (discussed in Chapter 5). However, in social work we rarely expect interventions to have homogeneous effects across samples and settings. Whether a review can explore possible moderators of effects depends on the number of studies in the analysis (and statistical power). Unfortunately most reviews are quite limited in this respect, due to the paucity of rigorous primary studies in many areas. When reviewers can examine potential sources of heterogeneity (with moderator analysis), their results are observational and tentative and do not support causal inferences. These findings can suggest directions for further research, including explicit studies of potential moderators.

Confidence Intervals

The interpretation of mean effects depends heavily on their CIs. It is important to note whether CIs cross the line of no effect and whether they include effects in a clinically significant range. When CIs cross the line of no effect, results are not statistically significant, and we can say that there is no evidence that the average effect is statistically different from zero. However, this is often misinterpreted: no evidence of an effect is *not* the same as evidence of no effect. In other words, null results do not prove that there is no effect; insufficient statistical power (too few studies, too much heterogeneity) is an alternative explanation for null results. If CIs also cover effect size (ES) values that are clinically significant, we cannot rule out the possibility that there is a clinically significant average effect that could not be detected in the analysis. If a power analysis suggests that the meta-analysis should have detected effects in a certain range but those effects are not apparent, then we have more evidence for rejecting the hypothesis of intervention effects.

The interpretation of null results should also take into account the nature of the counterfactual conditions in the primary studies. It is not appropriate to conclude that an intervention has "no effect" if the comparison is to another intervention (treatment as usual, for example). In this situation, it is proper to conclude that there is no evidence that the intervention of interest is more (or less) effective than another approach.

Point Estimates

As suggested above, an emphasis on point estimates is most appropriate when CIs do not cross the line of no effect; then we want to know the direction of effects and how large or small the effects may be. Summaries should state whether mean effects are positive, negative, or mixed (across outcomes) and give plain-language interpretations of ESs. The temptation to highlight those effects that are positive or statistically significant should be avoided in favor of a carefully balanced presentation of all results. ESs can be described as small, medium, or large using Cohen's standards (see Table 5.7). Alternatively, ESs can be interpreted using the binomial effect size display (described in Chapter 5; also see Lipsey & Wilson, 2001), by comparison to ESs detected in other meta-analyses, or with a simple but clear referent. Scher and colleagues (2006) used the latter approach, presenting pregnancy risks in terms of the percentages of cases likely to experience pregnancy outcomes in treated and comparison groups (see Fig. 1.1, Tables 6.1 and 6.2).

When Meta-Analysis is Not Used

Meta-analysis is not included in systematic reviews for several reasons. When there are less than two studies, it is simply not possible to compute a mean effect or perform any other meta-analytic routines. Generally, these reviews conclude that there was insufficient evidence to assess effects. They can also generate useful ideas about the types of studies that are needed.

If reviewers decide not to perform meta-analysis because they believe the studies are too weak or "too heterogeneous to combine," they should not pool results across studies using less rigorous techniques such as vote counting or a narrative synthesis. Too often, reviewers state that studies were too heterogeneous for meta-analysis, but then synthesize results anyway. Statements such as "most studies showed . . ." or "the evidence suggests . . ." are a product of some (usually unspecified) synthesis. When the methods used to generate such statements are not transparent, they do not belong in a systematic review.

Jeff Valentine (personal communication, June 2007) has suggested two alternatives. The first choice is to avoid drawing a conclusion about overall effects. In this case, reviewers may state that the results were too heterogeneous to combine, period. The second—less preferable—choice is to draw a conclusion based on a vote count of the *direction* of effects (not statistical significance) in the primary studies. This should always be accompanied by an explicit explanation of the process that was used and by caveats about the limitations of vote counting. Reviewers can present the data in Forest plots without mean effect estimates so readers can see how results were counted.

The Science of Research Synthesis and Implications for Social Work

This book has shown how systematic reviews and meta-analysis can allow researchers and consumers to digest large amounts of data and identify trends that may be obscured by sampling error and bias in individual studies. Although any method has limitations, systematic reviews and meta-analysis are simply the best tools available today for synthesizing quantitative findings from studies on related topics. Until better alternatives are devised, social worker scholars should use these methods to synthesize quantitative evidence on intervention effects and other topics.

There are many opportunities for systematic reviews and meta-analyses in social work. Reviewers can begin with their own questions and refine them based on a careful reading of previous work in the area. They can engage consumers, practitioners, and policy makers in discussions that will identify "burning questions" that may be translated into important topics for systematic reviews that may be useful for practice and policy. As suggested in Chapter 2, reviewers can join or form users' groups or create advisory boards to assist them in the developing the substantive topic for a review. Statistical and technical assistance can be obtained from experienced reviewers and meta-analysts or by registering a review with the Cochrane and/or Campbell Collaborations.

Alternatively, one could begin by reading existing narrative reviews and published meta-analyses to see whether a more systematic approach is warranted. As mentioned before, many of the reviews that undergird lists of evidence-based practices are not systematic or meta-analytic. Sometimes a fresh look at the prevailing wisdom produces surprising and important discoveries.

Perhaps empirical research will gain more prominence in social work and other helping professions, with the current emphasis on evidence-based practice. If so, opportunities for undertaking systematic reviews and meta-analyses may increase, hopefully in concert with much needed increases in support for primary research. To the extent that they improve transparency, accountability, and understanding of empirical evidence, systematic reviews and meta-analyses can make substantial contributions to the evidence base for social work practice and policy.

The future of research synthesis is bright. Meta-analysts are working on statistics for synthesis of single-subject designs, multivariate analysis (synthesizing regression coefficients, results of factor analysis), and methods for synthesizing data on diagnostic and prognostic accuracy of instruments. Methodological work has been undertaken to better understand the options available to reviewers and meta-analysts and the consequences of different choices. Global efforts to prevent publication and outcome reporting biases have been launched in health care and other fields. The science of research synthesis is rapidly advancing, and new developments will certainly arise.

Main Points: Chapter 7

- It is important to develop accurate and accessible (nontechnical) summaries of systematic reviews and meta-analyses. Plain-language summaries facilitate utilization of results.

- Meetings with policy makers, practitioners, consumers, and/or scholars can sharpen the presentation and interpretation of results.
- Interpretations of meta-analysis should consider the strength of the body of evidence, heterogeneity of effects, and confidence intervals as well as point estimates for mean effects.
- Interpretations of mean effects should consider whether confidence intervals include the line of no effect and/or values in a clinically significant range.
- When meta-analysis is not used, reviewers should avoid combining results across studies in a less rigorous way.
- Research synthesis allows us to digest large amounts of data and identify trends that may be obscured by sampling error and bias in individual studies. Systematic review methods and meta-analysis are the best tools for this purpose.
- There are many opportunities for research synthesis on important topics for social work and social welfare.
- The science of research synthesis is advancing at a rapid rate, and new developments are on the horizon.

For Further Reading

Cooper, H., Hedges, L. V., & Valentine, J. (in press). *Handbook of research synthesis* (2nd ed.). New York: Russell Sage Foundation.

Appendix A: AMSTAR (for assessment of multiple systematic reviews)

1. Was an a priori design provided? The research question and inclusion criteria should be established before the conduct of the review.	☐ Yes ☐ No ☐ Can't answer ☐ Not applicable
2. Was there duplicate study selection and data extraction? There should be at least two independent data extractors, and a consensus procedure for disagreements should be in place.	☐ Yes ☐ No ☐ Can't answer ☐ Not applicable
3. Was a comprehensive literature search performed? At least two electronic sources should be searched. The report must include years and databases used (e.g., Central, EMBASE, and MEDLINE). Key words and/or MeSH terms must be stated and, where feasible, the search strategy should be provided. All searches should be supplemented by consulting current contents, reviews, textbooks, specialized registers, or experts in the particular field of study and by reviewing the references in the studies found.	☐ Yes ☐ No ☐ Can't answer ☐ Not applicable
4. Was the status of publication (i.e., gray literature) used as an inclusion criterion? The authors should state that they searched for reports regardless of their publication type. The authors should state whether or not they excluded any reports (from the systematic review) based on their publication status, language, etc.	☐ Yes ☐ No ☐ Can't answer ☐ Not applicable

5. Was a list of studies (included and excluded) provided? A list of included and excluded studies should be provided.	☐ Yes ☐ No ☐ Can't answer ☐ Not applicable
6. Were the characteristics of the included studies provided? In an aggregated form such as a table, data from the original studies should be provided on the participants, interventions, and outcomes. The ranges of characteristics in all the studies analyzed (e.g. age, race, sex, relevant socioeconomic data, disease status, duration, severity, other diseases) should be reported.	☐ Yes ☐ No ☐ Can't answer ☐ Not applicable
7. Was the scientific quality of the included studies assessed and documented? A priori methods of assessment should be provided (e.g., for effectiveness studies if the author[s] chose to include only randomized, double-blind, placebo-controlled studies, or allocation concealment as inclusion criteria); for other types of studies, alternative items will be relevant.	☐ Yes ☐ No ☐ Can't answer ☐ Not applicable
8. Was the scientific quality of the included studies used appropriately in formulating conclusions? The results of the methodological rigor and scientific quality should be considered in the analysis and conclusions of the review and explicitly stated in the recommendations.	☐ Yes ☐ No ☐ Can't answer ☐ Not applicable
9. Were the methods used to combine the findings of studies appropriate? For the pooled results, a test should be done to ensure the studies were combinable, to assess their homogeneity (i.e., χ^2 test for homogeneity, I^2). If heterogeneity exists, a random-effects model should be used and/or the clinical appropriateness of combining should be taken into consideration (i.e., Is it sensible to combine?).	☐ Yes ☐ No ☐ Can't answer ☐ Not applicable
10. Was the likelihood of publication bias assessed? An assessment of publication bias should include a combination of graphical aids (e.g., funnel plot, other available tests) and/or statistical tests (e.g., Egger regression test).	☐ Yes ☐ No ☐ Can't answer ☐ Not applicable
11. Was the conflict of interest stated? Potential sources of support should be clearly acknowledged in both the systematic review and the included studies.	☐ Yes ☐ No ☐ Can't answer ☐ Not applicable

Source: Shea, Grimshaw, Wells, Boers, Andersson, Hamel, et al. (2007). Available at http://www.biomedcentral.com/content/supplementary/1471-2288-7-10-S1.doc.

Appendix B: Software for Systematic Reviews and Meta-Analysis

A number of software programs will support meta-analysis and other phases of the systematic review process. In this section, we describe some of these programs, although others are available.

Software for Systematic Reviews

RevMan. The Cochrane Collaboration's Review Manager (RevMan) runs on Windows operating systems and can be downloaded for free from http://www.cc-ims.net/RevMan. A free, downloadable manual and built-in help facility are available. RevMan is designed to handle several phases of the systematic review process, including protocol development, report writing, reference management, basic descriptive analyses, and meta-analysis. It is the required format for systematic reviews that are submitted to the Cochrane Database of Systematic Reviews.

RevMan includes an outline and word-processing facility for protocols and completed reviews. It provides templates for tables to describe included, excluded, and ongoing studies. It has a reference management facility with in-text links for citations. RevMan accommodates multiple comparisons and multiple outcomes in the same data sheet. It computes odds ratios and risk ratios for dichotomous data, and WMDs and SMDs (using Hedges' $\hat{g}$ to correct for small-sample bias) for continuous outcomes. Several formulas are available for inverse variance weights. RevMan can fit both fixed-effect and random-effects models. It provides Q and I^2 heterogeneity tests and produces Forest plots and funnel plots. Additional tables and graphs can be pasted in.

EPPI-Reviewer. Developed by the EPPI Centre, EPPI-Reviewer is a commercial, Web-based program that supports many phases of the systematic review process. It allows reviewers to import citations from major social sciences databases, create a permanent search log, and track the procurement status of each citation. Several reviewers can assign keywords to studies and extract data from included studies. The program includes a generic data extraction format that can be tailored for particular reviews. It calculates Cohen's κ for interrater reliability and reports potential discrepancies between coders. It can calculate SMDs from a wide range of published data, and it computes odds ratios, risk ratios, and risk differences from 2×2 tables. Categorical data can be displayed in frequencies and crosstabs. The program can produce Forest plots and it fits fixed effect and random effects meta-analysis. See http://www.eppi.org.uk/ and http://www.eppi.ioe.ac.uk/cms/Portals/0/PDF reviews and summaries/EPPI-Reviewer_Feb_06.pdf.

TrialStat SRS. SRS is a commercial, Web-based program that supports study eligibility decisions and data extraction. It allows reviewers to upload citations and abstracts from a reference management program (such as Endnote, Procite, or RefMan). Reviewers can track procurement status and attach full-text reports (in Word or PDF formats). Reviewers create forms for screening and data extraction. Screening and data extraction can be done in several stages, with decision rules attached to specific questions. The program monitors raters' progress, calculates Cohen's κ to assess interrater reliability on study eligibility decisions, and reports coding decisions and potential discrepancies. Results can be exported to Excel spreadsheets or Cochrane's RevMan. See www.trial stat.com.

Effect Size Calculators

David B. Wilson created a very useful set of Excel macros that can be used to calculate effect sizes (d and r) from a variety of statistics, including means, t-tests, proportions, frequencies, χ^2, and one-way ANOVA. This program also computes weighted means and pooled standard deviations, and converts d to r and vice versa. This program can be downloaded free of charge from http://mason.gmu.edu/~dwilsonb/ma.html (scroll down to es_calculator.zip).

Meta-Analysis with General Statistical Software Programs

Most of the statistical software packages that are used by social scientists (e.g., SAS, SPSS, and Stata) can produce basic statistics for meta-analysis. With the aid of macros written by meta-analysts, some of these programs will produce graphs and advanced statistics for meta-analysis.

David Wilson created a set of macros that can be used with SAS, SPSS, or Stata to perform a variety of meta-analytic analyses, mean effect size estimation (fixed-effect and random-effects models) with inverse variance weights, the Q test for heterogeneity, and moderator analysis with the analog to ANOVA, fixed-effect meta-regression, and random-effects meta-regression. Designed for use with Lipsey and Wilson's (2001) book *Practical Meta-Analysis,* these macros are available free of charge at http://mason.gmu.edu/~dwilsonb/ma.html.

Stata. Many add-in macros are available for conducting meta-analysis in Stata. These are continuously updated and relatively easy to use. Macros are available for inverse variance weighted meta-analysis, heterogeneity tests, meta-regression, funnel plots, tests of funnel plot asymmetry, trim-and-fill analysis, cumulative meta-analysis, NNT calculations, and other functions. Some of these routines use Stata's enhanced graphics capabilities. A menu-driven interface for meta-analysis macros is also now available. User-written macros are described at http://www.stata.com/support/faqs/stat/meta.html and can be downloaded by

Stata users (i.e., from within Stata) from the Stata Web site (www.stata .com). Also see Sterne, Bradburn, and Egger (2001).

SAS. See David Wilson's macros (described above) and Wang and Bushman (1999).

SPSS. See David Wilson's macros (described above).

WinBUGS/BUGS (Bayesian inference Using Gibbs Sampling) programs run Bayesian analyses of complex statistical models and can be used for meta-analysis. Responsible use of this free software requires understanding of Bayesian statistics. See http://www.mrc-bsu.cam.ac.uk/bugs/.

Commercial Programs for Meta-Analysis

Comprehensive Meta-Analysis (CMA). Probably the most sophisticated stand-alone software package for meta-analysis, CMA runs on Windows operating systems. Through a spreadsheet interface, it is possible to enter data for each study in its own format. CMA 2.0 accommodates multiple independent subgroups, outcomes, time points, or comparisons within studies in the same data sheet. Additionally, the software facilitates data analysis with different classes of data—continuous data, binary data, and correlations—and performs moderator analysis, mixed effects analysis of variance, and meta-regression. It produces high-quality Forest plots and allows for the control of all elements in the Forest plot. It has an excellent module for assessing heterogeneity, as well as publication bias. The program can be downloaded on a trial basis from www.meta-analysis .com.

MetaWin is another commercial software program for meta-analysis that runs on Windows operating systems. The program can produce several different effect sizes, including Hedges' $\hat{g}$, odds ratios and risk ratios, and Fisher's *z* transformation for correlations. It produces fixed-effect and random-effects models and conducts heterogeneity analysis, subgroup analysis, meta-regression, and cumulative meta-analysis. Resampling methods (different bootstrap procedures) are also available. The software displays funnel plots, scatter plots, histograms, and other graphics. See http://www.metawinsoft.com/.

Shareware

Meta-Stat is a DOS-based computer program that can be downloaded for free from http://ericae.net/meta/metastat.htm. The program facilitates coding of study features and effect size calculations. It produces corrected regression outputs, heterogeneity statistics, and variance ratios, and it displays data in a variety of charts.

EasyMA, another free software package for conducting meta-analysis; it is available at http://www.spc.univ-lyon1.fr/easyma.dos/. It is an MS-DOS program with a user-friendly interface developed to assist in the synthesis of binary data from clinical trials. It can fit both fixed- and random-effects models. The program produces a number of plots, such as the Forest plot, and includes the capacity to conduct subgroup analysis and cumulative meta-analysis. Limitations of EasyMA include its restriction to binary outcomes.

Mix (Meta-Analysis with Interactive eXplanations) is a free Excel-based program that is available at http://www.mix-for-meta-analysis .info/. This program is well suited for learning meta-analysis because it provides several examples along with data from a number of well-known books on meta-analysis. These data can be reanalyzed using various approaches. The program computes many effect size metrics for both categorical and continuous outcomes. Fixed-effect and random-effects models can be fitted. Using Excel-based tables and graphics, the program can display Forest plots and funnel plots.

Useful Web Sites

David B. Wilson's ES calculator; macros for meta-analysis with SAS, SPSS, and Stata; and slides from a professional development course on meta-analysis are available at http://mason.gmu.edu/~dwilsonb/ma .html.

Alexander J. Sutton's Web site contains reviews of software for meta-analysis. See http://www2.le.ac.uk/departments/health-sciences/ extranet/research-groups/biostatistics/ajs22/meta/.

William R. Shadish's Web site includes links (or references) to meta-analysis software, a list of meta-analyses of psychotherapy, information on meta-analysis for single-subject designs (datasets, methods, and an archive of meta-analyses of single-subject designs), and computer program for ES calculations. See http://faculty.ucmerced.edu/wshadish/ Meta-Analysis Links.htm.

Appendix C: Suggested Outline for Reporting Systematic Reviews and Meta-Analysis

Adapted from Higgins & Green (2006). Items indicated with * should be included in the protocol.

*1. Cover sheet: title, citation details, and contact addresses
2. Plain-language summary
3. Structured abstract
    3.1. Background
    3.2. Objectives
    3.3. Search strategy
    3.4. Selection criteria
    3.5. Data collection and analysis
    3.6. Main results
    3.7. Authors' conclusions
*4. Background
    4.1. Description of the problem/condition (importance, prevalence/incidence)
    4.2. Description of the intervention(s) of interest, their role in current practice
    4.3. How the intervention might work (logic model)
    4.4. Why the review is important

*5. Objectives of the review

*6. Methods sections

    6.1. Criteria for considering studies for this review

        6.1.1. Types of studies: thresholds for inclusion (based on study design and/or conduct), justification of any reasons for exclusion

        6.1.2. Types of participants: problems/diagnoses/conditions of interest, age groups and settings

        6.1.3. Types of interventions: experimental and control/comparison conditions, indicating central comparisons of interest; any restrictions on dose, frequency, intensity, or duration

        6.1.4. Types of outcome measures

            6.1.4.1. Primary outcomes

            6.1.4.2. Secondary outcomes

            6.1.4.3. Adverse outcomes

            6.1.4.4. Economic data

            6.1.4.5. Timing of outcome assessment

    6.2. Search strategy

        6.2.1. Electronic searches: bibliographic databases searched, dates and periods searched, any constraints such as language (full search strategies for each database are listed here or in an additional table)

        6.2.2. Gray literature sources, such as reports and conference proceedings

        6.2.3. Hand-searching (titles of journals hand-searched)

        6.2.4. Reference lists

        6.2.5. World Wide Web sites searched

        6.2.6. Personal correspondence

    6.3. Data collection and analysis methods

        6.3.1. Selection of studies: how selection criteria were applied, number of raters involved, how disagreements were handled

        6.3.2. Data extraction and management: method used to extract or obtain data from published reports or from

investigators, data extraction forms, number of raters
involved, how disagreements were resolved, methods
for processing data in preparation for analysis

6.3.3. Assessment of methodological quality of included
studies: method used, number of raters involved, how
disagreements were resolved, how results were used in
the interpretation of results

6.3.4. Measures of treatment effect: choices of effect size
metrics for:

6.3.4.1. Dichotomous data (e.g., odds ratio, risk ratio,
or risk difference)

6.3.4.2. Continuous data (e.g., weighted mean difference, standardized mean difference)

6.3.4.3. Time-to-event data (if applicable; e.g., hazard
rates)

6.3.5. Unit of analysis issues: how reviewers handled studies
with multiple treatment or comparison/control
groups, crossover trials, cluster randomized trials

6.3.6. Dealing with missing data on participants or outcomes: attempts to obtain missing data from investigators, methods for imputing missing data (if applicable), intention-to-treat analysis, methods for
handling missing statistics (e.g., means, SDs)

6.3.7. Assessment of heterogeneity: clinical/substantive heterogeneity, statistical heterogeneity

6.3.8. Assessment of reporting biases: how publication bias
and other potential biases are addressed (e.g., funnel
plots, statistical tests, imputation)

6.3.9. Data synthesis (meta-analysis): choice of fixed effect or
random effects model

6.3.10. Moderator analysis and investigation of heterogeneity: list a priori plans for subgroup analyses, meta-
regression

6.3.11. Sensitivity analysis: how reviewers tested whether
conclusions were robust to decisions made during the

review process (e.g., inclusion/exclusion of particular studies, imputing missing data, choice of a method for analysis)

7. Results sections

   7.1. Results of the search (lined to a QUOROM-type flowchart)

   7.2. Excluded studies and reasons for exclusion (linked to a table of specific reasons for inclusion for each study)

   7.3. Description of included studies: designs, sample sizes, setting, participants, interventions, outcomes (linked to a table that describes each study)

   7.4. Methodological quality of included studies: general quality of the included studies, variability in qualities across studies, any important flaws in individual studies (linked to a table showing how each study was rated on each of the following criteria)

      7.4.1. Allocation methods: allocation sequence generation, sequence concealment, judgments about risk of bias from allocation methods

      7.4.2. Blinding: who was blinded, judgments about risk of bias

      7.4.3. Follow-up and exclusions (attrition): completeness of data for each of the main outcomes, concerns about exclusion of participants and excessive (or differential) dropout

      7.4.4. Selective reporting: concerns about selective reporting of outcomes, time points, subgroups, or analyses

      7.4.5. Other potential sources of bias

   7.5. Main findings: organized by outcome measure (to address objectives of the review, rather than by individual studies; linked to statistical summary tables and graphs)

8. Discussion

   8.1. Summary of main results (benefits and harms)

   8.2. Overall completeness and applicability of evidence

   8.3. Quality of the evidence

   8.4. Potential biases in the review process

   8.5. Agreements and disagreements with other studies or reviews

Appendix D: Sample Search Strategy

Source: Macdonald, G. M., Higgins, J. P. T., & Ramchandani, P. (2006). Cognitive-behavioural interventions for children who have been sexually abused. In *Cochrane Database of Systematic Reviews*, 4. Also available at http://www.campbellcollaboration.org/doc-pdf/B9804CAMPBELL FINAL.PDF.

The following electronic databases were searched:

> Cochrane Central Register of Controlled Trials (CENTRAL) to Issue 3, 2005
> MEDLINE: 1966 to November 2005
> EMBASE: 1980 to November 2005
> CINAHL: 1982 to November 2005
> PsycINFO: 1887 to week 4 November 2005
> LILACS: 1982 to 2005
> SIGLE: 1980 to 2005

The full search strategies for all databases appear below. Appropriate trials filters were added to each strategy where necessary.

CENTRAL, published on the Cochrane Library, was searched to Issue 3, 2005, using the following terms:

#1 MeSH descriptor CHILD ABUSE explode trees 1, 2, and 3
#2 (CHILD* in All Text near/6 ABUSE* in All Text)
#3 (SEX* in All Text near/6 ABUSE* in All Text)
#4 MeSH descriptor INCEST explode tree 1
#5 INCEST* in All Text
#6 (SEX* in All Text near/6 OFFENC* in All Text)
#7 (SEX* in All Text near/6 CHILD* in All Text)
#8 (SEX* in All Text near/6 OFFENS* in All Text)
#9 (((((((#1 or #2) or #3) or #4) or #5) or #6) or #7) or #8)
#10 MeSH descriptor CHILD explode tree 1
#11 CHILD* in All Text
#12 INFANT* in All Text
#13 TEENAGE* in All Text
#14 ADOLESCEN* in All Text
#15 PRESCHOOL* in All Text
#16 PRE-SCHOOL* in All Text
#17 BABY in All Text
#18 BABIES in All Text
#19 ((((((((#10 or #11) or #12) or #13) or #14) or #15) or #16) or #17) or #18)
#20 (#19 and #9)
#21 MeSH descriptor PSYCHOTHERAPY explode tree 1
#22 PSYCHOTHERAP* in All Text
#23 THERAP* in All Text
#24 ((#21 or #22) or #23)
#25 (#20 and #24)

MEDLINE 1966 to November 2005

1 child abuse/ or child abuse, sexual/
2 (child$ adj5 abuse$).tw.
3 (sex$ adj5 abuse$).tw.

4 Incest/

5 incest$.tw.

6 (sex$ adj5 offenc$).tw.)

7 (sex$ adj5 child$).tw.

8 (sex$ adj5 offens$).tw.

9 or/1-8

10 adolescent/ or child/ or child, preschool/ or infant/

11 (child$ or infant$ or teenage$ or adolescen$ or preschool$ or pre-school$ or baby or babies).tw.

12 or/10-11)

13 Cognitive Therapy/

14 psychotherap$.tw.

15 therap$.tw.

16 or/13-15

17 9 and 12 and 16

CINAHL 1982 to November 2005

1 (child$ adj5 abuse$).tw.

2 (sex$ adj5 abuse$).tw.

3 incest$.tw.

4 (sex$ adj5 offenc$).tw.

5 (sex$ adj5 child$).tw.

6 (sex$ adj5 offens$).tw.

7 INCEST/

8 child abuse/ or child abuse, sexual/

9 or/1-8

10 adolescence/ or exp child/

11 (child$ or infant$ or teenage$ or adolescen$ or preschool$ or pre-school$ or baby or babies).tw.

12 or/10-11

13 COGNITIVE THERAPY/

14 psychotherap$.tw.

15 therap$.tw.

16 or/13-15
17 9 and 12 and 16

EMBASE 1980 to November 2005

1 (child$ adj5 abuse$).tw.
2 (sex$ adj5 abuse$).tw.
3 incest$.tw.
4 (sex$ adj5 offenc$).tw.
5 (sex$ adj5 child$).tw.
6 (sex$ adj5 offens$).tw.
7 incest/
8 Child Abuse/
9 or/1-8
10 Child/
11 adolescent/ or infant/
12 (child$ or infant$ teenage$ or adolescen$ or preschool$ or pre-school$ or baby or babies).tw.
13 or/10-12
14 psychotherapy/
15 psychotherap$.tw.
16 therap$.tw.
17 or/14-16
18 9 and 13 and 17

PsycINFO 1887 to Week 4 November 2005

#1 ("Child-Abuse" in MJ,MN)
#2 ((child* near abuse*) or (sex* near abuse*))
#3 ("Incest-" in MJ,MN)
#4 ((incest*) or (sex* near offenc*) or (sex* near child*))
#5 (sex* near offens*)
#6 ((sex* near offens*) or ((incest*) or (sex* near offenc*) or (sex* near child*)) or ("Incest-" in MJ,MN) or ((child* near abuse*) or (sex* near abuse*)) or ("Child-Abuse" in MJ,MN))

#7 ((child*) or (infant*) or (teenage*))

#8 ((adolescen*) or (preschool*) or (pre-school*))

#9 ((baby) or (babies))

#10 (((baby) or (babies)) or ((adolescen*) or (preschool*) or (pre-school*)) or ((child*) or (infant*) or (teenage*)))

#11 ("Cognitive-Behavior-Therapy" in MJ,MN)

#12 psychotherap*

#13 therap*

#14 ((therap*) or (psychotherap*) or ("Cognitive-Behavior-Therapy" in MJ,MN))

#15 ((therap*) or (psychotherap*) or ("Cognitive-Behavior-Therapy" in MJ,MN)) and (((baby)or(babies)) or ((adolescen*) or (preschool*) or (pre-school*)) or ((child*) or (infant*) or (teenage*))) and ((sex* near offens*) or ((incest*) or (sex* near offenc*) or (sex* near child*)) or ("Incest-" in MJ,MN) or ((child* near abuse*) or (sex* near abuse*)) or ("Child-Abuse" in MJ,MN))

SIGLE 1980 to November 2005

#1 (child* near abuse*) or (sex* near abuse*) or (incest*)

#2 (sex* near offenc*) or (sex* near child*) or (sex* near offens*)

#3 ((sex* near offenc*) or (sex* near child*) or (sex* near offens*)) or ((child* near abuse*) or (sex* near abuse*) or (incest*))

#4 (child*) or (infant*) or (teenage*)

#5 (adolescen*) or (preschool*) or (pre-school*)

#6 (baby) or (babies)

#7 ((adolescen*) or (preschool*) or (pre-school*)) or ((child*) or (infant*) or (teenage*)) or ((baby) or (babies))

#8 (psychotherap*) or (therap*)

#9 (((sex* near offenc*) or (sex* near child*) or (sex* near offens*)) or ((child* near abuse*) or (sex* near abuse*) or (incest*))) and ((psychotherap*) or (therap*)) and (((adolescen*) or (preschool*) or (pre-school*)) or ((child*) or (infant*) or (teenage*)) or ((baby) or (babies)))

LILACS 1982 to November 2005

((child$ abuse$) OR (sex$ abuse$) OR (incest$) or (sex$ offen$) OR
(sex$ child$)) [Words] and ((therap$) OR (psychotherap$) OR (cog-
nitiv$))

References in previous reviews and studies were also checked. Authors
and known experts were contacted to identify any additional or unpublished data. Efforts were made to establish contacts in countries in
which English is not the dominant language.

Appendix E: Screening and Data Extraction Form for Cochrane/Campbell Review of Effects of Multisystemic Therapy (MST)

Source: Littell, Campbell, Green, and Toews, 2007.

Level 1: Initial Screening

1. Is this paper about MST (perhaps in addition to other topics)?
   - Yes
   - No
   - Can't tell
2. What is this?
   - MST outcome evaluation
   - Review of MST outcome studies (and other research)
   - Descriptive, correlational, or case study
   - Theoretical or position paper, editorial, or book review
   - Practice guidelines or treatment manual
   - Can't tell

Level 2: Eligibility Decisions

1. Does this study include two or more parallel cohorts (groups that received different treatments and were assessed at the same points in time)?
   ○ Yes
   ○ No
   ○ Can't tell
2. Is it a randomized experiment?
   ○ Yes
   ○ No
   ○ Can't tell
3. Does this study include a licensed MST program?
   ○ Yes
   ○ No
   ○ Can't tell
4. Does it include youth (ages 10–17) with social, emotional, or behavioral problems?
   ○ Yes
   ○ No
   ○ Can't tell
5. Is the primary presenting problem a medical condition (diabetes or HIV-positive status)?
   ○ Yes
   ○ No
   ○ Can't tell

Level 3: Data Extraction: Study Level

Research methods

1. How were comparison/control groups formed?
   ○ Random assignment
   ○ Other (specify)
2. If random assignment, specify design
   ○ Simple/systematic (individuals/families)

- Stratified/blocked (identify stratifying variables)
- Yoked pairs (created by timing of enrollment into the study)
- Matched pairs (identify matching variables)
- Cluster (group) randomized
- Other (specify)
- Can't tell

3. Who performed group assignment?
   - Research staff
   - Program staff
   - Can't tell
   - Other (specify)

4. How was random assignment performed?
   - Computer generated
   - Random numbers table
   - Coins or dice
   - Other (describe)
   - Can't tell

5. How many separate sites were included in the study?
   - One
   - Two
   - Three
   - Four
   - Five or more

6. Was random assignment performed in the same way in all sites?
   - Yes
   - No (explain)
   - Can't tell

7. How many intervention groups were there? (MST counts as one)
   - One (MST)
   - Two (MST plus what?)
   - Three (MST plus what?)

8. How many intervention groups are relevant for this review?
   - One (MST)
   - More than one (explain)

9. How many *different* control/comparison groups were there (i.e., groups that received different treatments, not counting multiple sites)?
   ◦ One
   ◦ Two or more (explain)
10. How many control/comparison groups are relevant for this review?
    ◦ One
    ◦ More than one (explain)

Settings

11. Location of interventions (check all that apply)
    ◦ Urban
    ◦ Suburban
    ◦ Rural
    ◦ Can't tell

Samples

12. Location details (city, state, country)
13. Primary service sector
    ◦ Juvenile justice
    ◦ Mental Health
    ◦ Child Welfare
    ◦ Other (specify)
14. Sample size

Number of cases	MST	Control	Total	Pg# & Notes
Referred to study				
Consented				
Randomly assigned				
Started treatment				
Completed treatment				
Completed post-tx data				
Completed follow-up				

15. Sample characteristics

	MST	Control	Total	Pg# & Notes
Gender (e.g., % male)				
Youth ages				
Race/ethnicity				
Socio economic status				
Family composition				
Other sample characteristics				

16. Were there any differences between program and control groups at baseline?
    ○ Yes (describe differences)
    ○ No (how do we know?)
    ○ Can't tell
17. Was there any analysis of differences between MST program completers and dropouts?
    ○ Yes
    ○ No
    ○ Can't tell
18. What were the differences between MST program completers and drop-outs?
19. Was there any analysis of differences between completers and drop-outs *in the control group?*
20. What were the differences between completers and drop-outs *in the control group?*

Services

21. MST Service Characteristics

	Min	Max	Mean	SD	Pg# & Notes
Duration in					
○ Days					
○ Weeks					
Months					
Hours of contact					
○ Per week					
○ Per month					
Other (explain)					
Total hours of contact					

22. Other characteristics of MST services
23. Characteristics of MST staff (education, demographics, etc.)
24. Describe methods used to insure quality of MST services (supervision, training, consultation)
25. Is there any information on program adherence (fidelity) to MST?
    ○ Yes (describe)
    ○ No
    ○ Not sure
26. Were TAM scores used/reported?
    ○ Used and reported (give results)
    ○ Used but not reported
    ○ Can't tell
    ○ Not used
27. Were there any implementation differences between sites? (TAM scores OR any qualitative/quantitative differences)
    ○ Yes (describe differences)
    ○ No (how do we know?)
    ○ Can't tell

28. Is information on MST program costs provided?
   ◦ Cost per case
   ◦ Total cost
   ◦ No info

Services provided to control cases

29. Type of control group
   ◦ Usual services (treatment as usual)
   ◦ Alternative service (describe)
   ◦ No service
30. Describe services provided to control group
31. Characteristics of staff who provided services to control cases (education, demographics, etc.)

Level 4: Outcome measures

1. When were data collected? (check all that apply)
   ◦ Baseline
   ◦ Post-tx
   ◦ 1st follow-up (when?)
   ◦ 2nd follow-up (when?)
   ◦ 3rd follow-up (when?)
   ◦ 4th follow-up (when?)
   ◦ 5th follow-up (when?)
   ◦ Other
2. Who conducted interviews?
   ◦ Research staff
   ◦ Program staff
   ◦ Both
   ◦ No interviews
3. Were data collected in the same manner for MST tx and control groups?
   ◦ Yes
   ◦ No (what were the differences?)
   ◦ Can't tell

Outcome measures

Instructions: Please enter outcome measures in the order in which they are described in the report. Note that a single outcome measure can be completed by multiple sources and at multiple points in time (data from specific sources and time-points will be entered later).

#	Topic	Reliability & Validity	Format	Direction	Source	Mode Admin	Blind?	Pg# & notes
1	Code: Definition:	Info from: ○ Other samples ○ This sample ○ Unclear Info provided:	○ Dichotomy ○ Continuous	High score or event is ○ Positive ○ Negative ○ Can't tell	○ Youth ○ Parent ○ Teacher ○ Clinician ○ Admin data ○ Other ○ Unclear	○ Self-admin ○ Interview ○ Other	○ Yes ○ No ○ Can't tell	

Topic codes (from drop down menus): Placed (jail/hospital/foster), Arrest/convict, Delinquent, Drug/alc use, Youth psych symptoms, Social skills/peer relations, School attend, Parent psych symptoms, Family functioning, Parental supervision, Service use, Other

Note: row repeats as often as necessary to code all measures.

Outcome data

Please enter outcome data in the tables provided below. Enter dichotomous outcomes first, then continuous outcomes. Outcome # refers to the measures described above.

Dichotomous outcome data

Enter data only if it is provided (do not perform calculations). OR = odds ratio. Enter exact *p* value if available. If covariates (control variables) are used in the analysis, please identify these variables under Statistics (cov).

Outc #	Timing	Source	Valid Ns	n w/ event	% w event	Statistics	Pg# & notes
	○ Post tx	○ youth	MST	MST	MST	OR	
	○ 1st f-u	○ parent				95% CI	
	○ 2nd f-u	○ teacher				χ^2	
	○ 3rd f-u	○ clinician	Control	Control	Control	Df	
	○ 4th f-u	○ admin data				*p* val	
	○ 5th f-u	○ other				Other	
	○ Other					Cov	

*Repeated as often as needed

Continuous outcome data

If change/gain scores are provided, enter under "other data." If covariates (control variables) are used in the analysis, please identify these variables under Statistics (cov).

Outc #	Timing	Source	Valid Ns	Means	SDs	Statistics	Pg# & notes
	○ Post tx	○ youth	MST	MST	MST	p	
	○ 1st f-u	○ parent				t	
	○ 2nd f-u	○ teacher				F	
	○ 3rd f-u	○ clinician	Control	Control	Control	df	
	○ 4th f-u	○ admin data				ES	
	○ 5th f-u	○ other				Other	
	○ Other					Cov	

*Repeated as often as needed

Level 5: Study quality standards

1. **Random generation of allocation** (assignment) to groups (explicitly stated use of either computer-generated random numbers, table of random numbers, drawing lots or envelopes, coin tossing, shuffling cards, or throwing dice)
   ○ Met
   ○ Unclear
   ○ Unmet

2. **Allocation concealment** (participants and investigators cannot foresee assignment; e.g., central randomization performed at site remote from trial location or monitored use of sequentially numbered, sealed, opaque envelopes)
   ○ Met
   ○ Unclear
   ○ Unmet

3. Avoidance of **performance bias** (no treatment differences between groups other than the main intervention contrasts)
   ○ Met
   ○ Unclear
   ○ Unmet

4. Avoidance of **attrition bias** (losses to follow-up less than or equal to 20% and equally distributed between comparison groups)
   ○ Met for all outcomes
   ○ Met for some outcomes
   ○ Unclear
   ○ Unmet

5. Avoidance of **detection bias** (assessor unaware of the assigned treatment when collecting outcome measures)
   ○ Met for all outcomes
   ○ Met for some outcomes
   ○ Unclear
   ○ Unmet

6. **Intention to treat** (data analysed according to assigned group whether or not assigned services were received/completed)
   - Met for all outcomes
   - Met for some outcomes
   - Unclear
   - Unmet

7. **Standardized observation periods** (follow-up data were collected from each case at a fixed point in time after random assignment)
   - Met for all outcomes
   - Met for some outcomes
   - Unclear
   - Unmet

8. **Validated outcome measures** (use of instruments with demonstrated reliability and validity in this sample or similar samples OR use of public agency administrative data, behavioral, or biologic measures)
   - Met for all outcomes
   - Met for some outcomes
   - Unclear
   - Unmet

9. **Conflicts of interest** (researchers or data collectors would benefit if results favored MST OR the control group)
   - Clear conflict of interest (explain)
   - Possible conflict of interest (explain)
   - Conflict of interest is unlikely (explain)
   - Unclear

10. **Allegiance bias:** Is there any indication that researchers believed that MST was better/worse than the alternatives before the study began?
    - Yes (explain)
    - No (explain)
    - Can't tell

11. **Comments:**

_____

_____

_____

_____

_____

_____

_____

_____

_____

_____

Glossary

Absolute risk reduction (ARR): see *Risk difference*

Allocation: the assignment of a participant (individual or group) to one of the conditions (arms) of a study, such as an intervention, comparison, or control condition

Allocation bias: see *Selection bias*

Allocation concealment: methods used to prevent the prediction or alternation of allocation sequences. If the allocation sequence can be foreseen, it can be manipulated or altered, which compromises randomization; reduces selection bias. (In contrast, *blinding* refers to lack of knowledge of allocation during assessment or measurement.)

Arm (of a study): one of the conditions in a clinical trial

Attrition: loss of study participants after their enrollment (or random assignment) in a study

Attrition bias: systematic differences between participants who remain in treatment and those who drop out; systematic differences between those who continue in the study and those who withdraw; systematic differences between the treatment and control/comparison groups in dropouts or withdrawals that alter the original composition of the groups

Bias: systematic error in an estimate or inference; produces a consistent overestimation or underestimation of effects

Binary data: dichotomous variables that are coded 0 or 1 (0 often represents the absence of a characteristic, 1 represents its presence)

Blinding (masking): concealing information about the type of treatment provided to specific participants. Blinding may be applied to study participants and/or data collection staff (if both, the study is *double-blind*). This reduces performance and detection biases.

Comparison group: a group that is compared with a treatment group and receives either another treatment or no treatment

Confidence interval (CI): range of values likely to include the true effect (or true value of a population parameter). CIs express the level of certainty associated with a parameter estimate. A parameter estimate with a narrow CI is more precise (more likely to be an accurate estimate of the population parameter) than one with a wide interval. Typically, 95% CIs are calculated (95% of the independent, random samples from a population would produce estimates that lie in this range).

Confirmation bias: the tendency to emphasize evidence that supports a hypothesis and ignore evidence to the contrary

Confound: an extraneous variable that is correlated with the variable of interest

Control group: a comparison group that does not receive a treatment and is instead assigned to a no-treatment condition, a waiting list for treatment, or a placebo control condition

Controlled clinical trial (CCT): a study that compares two or more treatment conditions using a quasi-random method of allocation (e.g., birthdates or record numbers) or an allocation method that is possibly random (or possibly quasi-random) but not clearly described

Continuous variable: can take on a range of values that can be expressed on a numeric scale

Counterfactual: what would have happened in the absence of exposure to a causal factor

Detection bias: systematic differences between groups in the collection of outcome data

Dichotomous variable: has only two categories and is often used to express the presence or absence of a characteristic or event

Effect size: a measure of the magnitude (strength) and direction of a relationship between variables

Effectiveness: impact of a treatment under real-world conditions

Efficacy: impact of a treatment under ideal conditions

Evidence-based practice: integration of the best available research evidence with clinical expertise and client values to make informed decisions in individual cases

Evidence-based policy: integration of the best available research evidence with expertise and consumer values to make informed policy decisions

External validity: extent to which results of a study apply to other participants, settings, applications, and measurements; the credibility of inferences that involve generalization or extrapolation of results

Fixed effect model: An approach for estimating mean effects that assumes all studies come from a population in which there is one true effect that does not vary (the effect is fixed across studies). Between-study variation is expected to be due to sampling error alone and is ignored. Weights are assigned to studies based solely on within-study variance (inverse variance methods). (Compare to *random effects model.*)

Forest plot: a visual display of effect sizes and confidence intervals from one or more studies

Funnel plot: A graphical method for detecting publication bias, other sources of bias, and small-sample effects; based on the assumption that study effect sizes are normally distributed around the mean effect. In the absence of bias, the distribution of effect sizes will be small at the top of the plot (where more precise estimates are shown) and wider at the bottom.

Hedges' ĝ: an effect size metric for continuous variables, similar to the standardized mean difference, that includes an adjustment for small-sample bias

Heterogeneity: the extent of variation in a distribution of effect sizes. Includes differences between studies in terms of outcomes (statistical heterogeneity), populations (clinical heterogeneity), and methods (methodological differences).

Homogeneity: the similarity of results across studies; the assumption (in a fixed-effect model) that all studies are from the same population, and each study-level effect size is an estimate of a single population parameter

Intention to treat (ITT): analysis of experimental data in which participants remain in the group to which they were originally assigned, regardless of whether they received that treatment. This preserves the benefits of random assignment.

Internal validity: the credibility of inferences about a causal relationship between variables. In a study of treatment effects, this is the extent to which observed outcomes can be attributed to intervention versus other factors.

Intraclass correlation coefficient (ICC): a set of indices of reliability for continuous variables, expressed as a ratio of the variance of interest over the sum of the variance of interest plus error. This allows researchers to assess the magnitude of different sources of variance in the measure, using the analysis of variance.

Inverse variance methods: weighting methods in which studies with more precise estimates (smaller confidence intervals) contribute more to the overall estimate than those with wider confidence intervals. The inverse variance is one divided by the square of the standard error.

Kappa (Cohen's kappa): a set of indices of interrater reliability for categorical variables, defined as a proportion of agreement that does not include the proportion of agreement that is expected due to chance alone

Log odds ratio: the natural logarithm of the odds ratio

MeSH terms: medical subject headings used in the MEDLINE and EMBASE databases to find studies on certain topics

Meta-analysis: statistical techniques used to analyze and synthesize results of multiple studies on the same topic

Meta-regression: a statistical analysis, similar to multiple regression, in which the potential impact of one or more continuous variables is assessed on a dependent variable; in this case the dependent variable is an effect size

Moderator analysis: procedures used to assess the influence of participant, treatment, or study design characteristics on variations in effect size. These include an analog to the analysis of variance and meta-regression.

Number needed to harm (NNH): the number of people who would need to be treated to produce one additional harmful outcome

Number needed to treat (NNT): the number of people who would require treatment to prevent one deleterious outcome; it is defined as the inverse of the *risk difference* (RD)

Odds: a probability value divided by its complement—that is, the chance that an event will occur divided by the chance that the event will not occur

Odds ratio (OR): a ratio of two odds values; for instance, the odds that an event will occur in one group compared with the odds that it will happen in another group

Outcome reporting bias: the tendency to report more information about statistically significant results than null results

Performance bias: systematic differences in the care provided to groups apart from the interventions under investigation (e.g., expectancy effects, additional enhancements, or contamination of treatments)

Point estimate: an observed value that is used to estimate the real value of the parameter (i.e., an effect or phenomenon of interest) in a larger population. Point estimates are accompanied by confidence intervals.

Power: see *Statistical power*

Precision: refers to the confidence one can place in a point estimate; estimates with smaller confidence intervals are more precise

Protocol: plan for a study that is developed in advance. A protocol for a systematic review and/or meta-analysis describes methods and procedures that will be used.

Publication bias: selection procedures that produce systematic differences between published and unpublished studies; usually refers to the increased likelihood of publication of statistically significant results and the systematic underrepresentation of null and negative results in the published literature

p value: from statistical significance tests, refers to the probability of a Type I error (rejecting the null hypothesis when the null hypothesis is true)

Quasi-experiment: study that tests effects of an intervention (or experimental manipulation) without using random assignment to create groups

Random assignment: using chance to allocate participants to treatment and comparison or control conditions. The purpose is to eliminate selection bias and most threats to internal validity, so that between-group differences on outcomes are likely due to treatment conditions and not to other factors.

Random effects model: a statistical model that includes both within-group sampling error and between-study variance in the computation of mean effects and confidence intervals. In contrast to fixed-effect modeling, this method of pooling effect sizes is based on the assumption that there is no single true effect in the population; instead, true effects are distributed (vary) across samples and studies.

Random error: measurement or sampling error due to chance (as opposed to systematic error)

Randomization: see *Random assignment*

Randomized controlled trial (RCT): a comparative study in which participants are allocated to experimental and comparison or control conditions purely by chance, and then outcomes for each group are compared in order to identify causal relationships between interventions and outcomes

Risk difference (RD) (also called the *absolute risk reduction [ARR]*): the risk (probability) that an event will occur in one group minus the risk of that event in another group

Risk ratio (RR) (also called *relative risk*): A ratio of the probability of an event in one group over the probability of the event in another group

Sampling error: the difference between a sample statistic and the population parameter it estimates

Selection bias: systematic differences between treatment and comparison/control (other than interventions under investigation) that relate to outcomes

Sensitivity analysis: comparing two or more models to determine whether results are robust (consistent) under different assumptions; often used to test the impacts of decisions made during the analysis

Standardized mean difference (SMD): a common measure of effect size. SMD is the difference between two group means, divided by their pooled standard deviation. It is also known as Cohen's *d*.

Statistical power: ability to detect effects (or differences) when they exist. Inverse of β, the probability of a Type II error.

Subgroup analysis: method to estimate effect sizes for certain groups that are subsets of the population of interest

Systematic error: see *Bias*

Systematic review: a comprehensive, unbiased, and reproducible review of prior studies that follows a detailed protocol (plan). This involves a clearly formulated research question, explicit inclusion and exclusion criteria, systematic methods to comprehensively identify relevant studies, interrater agreement on key decisions and coding, critical appraisal of the quality of evidence, and analysis and synthesis of data collected from the studies.

Variance: a measure of dispersion, indicating how widely values are spread around a mean or population parameter

References

Ahnert, L., Pinquart, M., & Lamb, M. E. (2006). Security of children's relationships with nonparental care providers: A meta-analysis. *Child Development*, *77*, 664–679.

Allen, M., & Burrell, N. (1996). Comparing the impact of homosexual and heterosexual parents on children: Meta-analysis of existing research. *Journal of Homosexuality*, *32*, 19–35.

Altman, D. G. (2001). Systematic reviews of evaluations of prognostic variables. *British Medical Journal*, *323*, 224–228.

Anderson, L. M., Charles, J. S., Fullilove, M. T., Scrimshaw, S. C., Fielding, J. E., Normand, J., et al. (2003). Providing affordable family housing and reducing residential segregation by income: A systematic review. *American Journal of Preventive Medicine*, *24*(3S), 47–67.

Anderson, L. M., Scrimshaw, S. C., Fullilove, M. T., Fielding, J. E., Normand, J., & the Task Force on Community Preventive Services. (2003). Culturally competent healthcare systems: A systematic review. *American Journal of Preventive Medicine*, *24*(3S), 68–79.

Anderson, L. M., Shinn, C., Fullilove, M. T., Scrimshaw, S. C., Fielding, J. E., Normand, J., et al. (2003). The effectiveness of early childhood development programs: A systematic review. *American Journal of Preventive Medicine*, *24*(3S), 32–46.

Barak, M. E., Nissly, J. A., & Levin, A. (2001). Antecedents to retention and turnover among child welfare, social work, and other human service employees: What can we learn from past research? A review and meta-analysis. *Social Service Review*, *75*, 625–661.

Bates, S., & Coren, E. (2006). *The extent and impact of parental mental health problems on families and the acceptability, accessibility and effectiveness of interventions.* London: Social Care Institute for Excellence (SCIE). Retrieved July 31, 2007, from http://www.scie.org.uk/publications/map/map01.pdf.

Becker, B. J. (2005). Failsafe *N* or file-drawer number. In H. R. Rothstein, A. J. Sutton, & M. Bornstein (Eds.), *Publication bias in meta-analysis: Prevention, assessment and adjustment* (pp. 111–125). West Sussex, England: John Wiley & Sons.

Becker, B. J., Hedges, L., & Pigott, T. D. (2004). *Campbell Collaboration statistical analysis policy brief.* Retrieved June 12, 2006, from http://www.camp bellcollaboration.org/MG/StatsPolicyBrief.pdf.

Begg, C. B. (1994). Publication bias. In H. Cooper & L. V. Hedges (Eds.), *The handbook of research synthesis* (pp. 399–409). New York: Russell Sage Foundation.

Bloom, H. S., Michalopoulos, C., Hill, C. J., & Lei, Y. (2002). *Can nonexperimental comparison group methods match the findings from a random assignment evaluation of mandatory welfare-to-work programs?* Retrieved January 2, 2007, from http://www.mdrc.org/publications/66/full.pdf.

Borenstein, M. (2005). Software for publication bias. In H. R. Rothstein, A. J. Sutton, & M. Borenstein (Eds.), *Publication bias in meta-analysis: Prevention, assessment and adjustments* (pp. 193–220). West Sussex, UK: John Wiley & Sons.

Borenstein, M., Hedges, L., & Rothstein, H. (2007). *Meta-analysis: Fixed effect vs random effects.* Retrieved October 10, 2007, from www.Meta-Analysis.com.

Bradley, M. C., & Mandell, D. (2005). Oppositional defiant disorder: A systematic review of evidence of intervention effectiveness. *Journal of Experimental Criminology*, *1*, 343–365.

Bushman, B. J., & Wells, G. L. (2001). Narrative impressions of literature: The availability bias and the corrective properties of meta-analytic approaches. *Personal and Social Psychology Bulletin*, *27*, 1123–1130.

Caetano, P. (2004). Standards for reporting non-randomized evaluations of behavioral and public health interventions: The TREND statement. *Society for the Study of Addiction*, *99*, 1075–1080.

Carlton, P. L., & Strawderman, W. E. (1996). Evaluating cumulated research I: The inadequacy of traditional methods. *Biological Psychiatry*, *39*, 65–72.

Chalmers, I., Hedges, L. V., & Cooper, H. (2002). A brief history of research synthesis. *Evaluation & the Health Professions*, *25*, 12–37.

Chan, A. W., Hróbjartsson, A., Haar, M. T., Gøtzsche, P. C., & Altman, D. G. (2004). Empirical evidence for selective reporting of outcomes in randomized trials: Comparison of protocols to published articles. *Journal of the American Medical Association, 291*, 2457–2465.

Clarke, A. T. (2006). Coping with interpersonal stress and psychosocial health among children and adolescents: A meta-analysis. *Journal of Youth and Adolescence, 35*, 11–24.

Cohen, J. (1969). *Statistical power analysis for the behavioral sciences.* New York: Academic Press.

Cohen, J. (1988). *Statistical power analysis for behavioral sciences* (2nd ed.). Hillsdale, NY: Lawrence Erlbaum Associates.

Cooper, H. (1998). *Synthesizing research* (3rd ed.). Thousand Oaks, CA: SAGE.

Cooper, H., & Hedges, L. V. (1994). *Handbook of research synthesis.* New York: Russell Sage Foundation.

Corcoran, J., & Dattalo, P. (2006). Parent involvement in treatment for ADHD: A meta-analysis of the published studies. *Research in Social Work Practice, 16*, 561–570.

Corcoran, J., & Pillai, V. K. (2007). Effectiveness of secondary pregnancy prevention programs: A meta-analysis. *Research on Social Practice, 17*, 5–18.

Cummings, S. R., Browner, W. S., & Hulley, S. B. (1988). Conceiving the research question. In S. B. Hulley & S. R. Cummings (Eds.), *Designing clinical research: An epidemiological approach* (pp. 12–17). Baltimore: Williams & Wilkins.

Cwikel, J., Behar, L., & Rabson-Hare, J. (2000). A comparison of a vote count and a meta-analysis review of intervention research with adult cancer patients. *Research on Social Work Practice, 10*, 139–158.

Deeks, J. J., Dinnes, J., D'Amico, R., Sowden, A. J., Sakarovitch, C., Song, F., et al. (2003). Evaluating non-randomised intervention studies. *Health Technology Assessment, 7*(27).

Deeks, J. J., Higgins, J. T. P., & Altman, D. (Eds.) (2006). Analysing and presenting results. In J. P. T. Higgins & S. Green (Eds.), *Cochrane Handbook for Systematic Reviews of Interventions* 4.2.6 [updated September 2006]; Section 8. In *The Cochrane Library, Issue 4, 2006.* Chichester, UK: John Wiley & Sons.

De Smidt, G. A., & Gorey, K. M. (1997). Unpublished social work research: Systematic replication of a recent meta-analysis of published intervention effectiveness research. *Social Work Research, 21*, 58–62.

Dickersin, K. (2005). Publication bias: Recognizing the problem, understanding its origins and scope, and preventing harm. In H. R. Rothstein, A. J. Sutton, & M. Bornstein (Eds.), *Publication bias in meta-analysis: Prevention, assessment, and adjustments* (pp. 11–33). Chichester, UK: John Wiley & Sons.

Duval, S. (2005). The trim and fill method. In H. R. Rothstein, A. J. Sutton, & M. Bornstein (Eds.), *Publication bias in meta-analysis: Prevention, assessment and adjustments* (pp. 128–144). West Sussex: John Wiley & Sons.

Dynarski, M., James-Burdumy, S., Mansfield, W., Mayer, D., Moore, M., Mullens, J., et al. (2001). *A broader view: The national evaluation of the 21st Century Community Learning Centers program.* Princeton, NJ: Mathematica Policy Research.

Eagly, A., Karau, S., & Makhijani, M. (1995). Gender and the effectiveness of leaders: A meta-analysis. *Psychological Bulletin, 117,* 125–145.

Egger, M., & Smith, G. D. (1998). Bias in location and selection of studies. *British Medical Journal, 316,* 61–66.

Egger, M., Smith, G. D., & Phillips, A. N. (1997). Meta-analysis: Principles and procedures. *British Medical Journal, 315,* 1533–1537.

Egger, M., Smith, G. D., Schneider, M., & Minder, C. (1997). Bias in meta-analysis detected by a simple, graphical test. *British Medical Journal, 315,* 629–634.

Egger, M., Zellweger-Zahner, T., Schneider, M., Junker, C., Lengeler, C., & Antes, G. (1997). Language bias in randomised controlled trials published in English and German. *The Lancet, 350,* 326–329.

Fischer, J. (1973). Is casework effective: A review. *Social Work,* January, 5–30.

Fischer, J. (1990). Problems and issues in meta-analysis. In L. Videka-Sherman & W. J. Reid (Eds.), *Advances in clinical social work research* (pp. 297–325). Silver Spring, MD: National Association of Social Workers.

Fraser, M. W., Nelson, K. E., & Rivard, J. C. (1997). Effectiveness of family preservation services. *Social Work Research, 21,* 138–153.

Gambrill, E. (2006). Evidence-based practice and policy: Choices ahead. *Research on Social Work Practice, 16,* 338–357.

Gibbs, L. E. (2003). *Evidence-based practice for the helping professions: A practical guide with integrated multimedia.* Pacific Grove, CA: Brooks/Cole-Thompson Learning.

Gibbs, L., & Gambrill, E. (2002). Evidence-based practice: Counterarguments to objections. *Research on Social Work Practice, 12,* 452–476.

Gilbody, S., Bower, P., Fletcher, J., Richards, D., & Sutton, A. J. (2006). Collaborative care for depression: A cumulative meta-analysis and review of longer-term outcomes. *Archives of Internal Medicine, 166,* 2314–2321.

Glasman, L. R., & Albarracin, D. (2006). Forming attitudes that predict future behavior: A meta-analysis of the attitude-behavior relation. *Psychological Bulletin, 132,* 778–822.

Glass, G., McGaw, B., & Smith, M. L. (1981). *Meta-analysis in social research.* Beverly Hills: SAGE Publications.

Glass, G. V. (1976). Primary, secondary, and meta-analysis of research. *Educational Researcher, 5,* 3–8.

Glass, G. V., & Smith, M. K. (1978). Meta-analysis of research on the relationship of class size and achievement. *Educational Evaluation and Policy Analysis, 1,* 2–16.

Glasziou, P., Irwig, L., Bain, C., & Colditz, G. (2001). *Systematic reviews in health care*. Cambridge, UK: Cambridge University Press.

Glazerman, S., Levy, D. M., & Myers, D. (2002). *Nonexperimental replications of social experiments: A systematic review*. Princeton, NJ: Mathematica Policy Research.

Gorey, K. M., Thyer, B. A., & Pawluck, D. E. (1998). Differential effectiveness of prevalent social work practice models: A meta-analysis. *Social Work, 43*, 269–278.

Gøtzsche, P. C., Hrógjartsson, A., Marić, K., & Tendal, B. (2007). Data extraction errors in meta-analyses that use standardized mean differences. *Journal of the American Medical Association, 298*, 430–437.

GRADE Working Group. (2004). Grading quality of evidence and strength of recommendations. *British Medical Journal, 328*, 1490–1497.

Grenier, A. M., & Gorey, K. M. (1998). The effectiveness of social work with older people and their families: A meta-analysis of conference proceedings. *Social Work Research, 22*, 60–64.

Hedges, L. (1990). Directions for future methodology. In K. W. Wachter & M. L. Straf (Eds.), *The future of meta-analysis* (pp. 11–26). New York: Russell Sage Foundation.

Hedges, L., Laine, R., & Greenwald, R. (1994). Does money matter? A meta-analysis of studies of the effects of differential school inputs on student outcomes. *Educational Research, 23*, 5–14.

Hedges, L. V. (1981). Distribution theory for Glass's estimator of effect size and related estimators. *Journal of Educational Statistics, 7*, 119–128.

Hedges, L. V., & Olkin, I. (1985). *Statistical methods for meta-analysis*. Orlando, FL: Academic Press.

Hedges, L. V., & Pigott, T. D. (2001). The power of statistical tests in meta-analysis. *Psychological Methods, 6*, 2003–2217.

Hedges, L. V., & Vevea, J. (2005). Selection methods approaches. In H. R. Rothstein, A. J. Sutton, & M. Bornstein (Eds.), *Publication bias in meta-analysis: Prevention, assessment and adjustments* (pp. 145–174). West Sussex, UK: John Wiley & Sons.

Henggeler, S. W., Rowland, M. D., Randall, J., Ward, D. M., Pickrel, S. G., Cunningham, P. B., et al. (1999). Home-based Multisystemic Therapy as an alternative to the hospitalization of youths in psychiatric crisis: Clinical outcomes. *Journal of the American Academy of Child and Adolescent Psychiatry, 38*, 1331–1339.

Herbison, P., Hay-Smith, J., & Gillespie, W. J. (2006). Adjustment of meta-analyses on the basis of quality scores should be abandoned. *Journal of Clinical Epidemiology, 59*, 1249–1256.

Higgins, J. P., Thompson, S. G., Deeks, J. J., & Altman, D.G. (2003). Measuring inconsistency in meta-analysis. *British Medical Journal, 327*, 557–560.

Higgins, J. P. T., & Green, S. (Eds.) (2006). *Cochrane handbook for systematic reviews of interventions.* Chichester, UK: John Wiley & Sons.

Hittner, J. B., & Swickert, R. (2006). Sensation seeking and alcohol use: A meta-analytic review. *Addictive Behaviors, 31*, 1383–1401.

Hodge, D. R. (2007). A systematic review of the empirical literature on intercessory prayer. *Research on Social Work Practice, 17*, 174–187.

Holden, G. (1991). The relationship of self efficacy appraisals to subsequent health related outcomes: A meta-analysis. *Social Work in Health Care, 16*, 53.

Hopewell, S., Clarke, M., Lefebvre, C., & Scherer, R. (2006). Handsearching versus electronic searching to identify reports of randomized trials. *The Cochrane Database of Systematic Reviews, 4.* Chichester, UK: John Wiley & Sons.

Hopewell, S., Clarke, M., & Mallett, S. (2005). Grey literature and systematic reviews. In H. R. Rothstein, A. J. Sutton, & M. Borenstein (Eds.), *Publication bias in meta-analysis: Prevention, assessment and adjustments* (pp. 49–72). West Sussex, England: John Wiley & Sons.

Hopewell, S., Clarke, M., Stewart, L., & Tierney, J. (2001). Time to publication for results of clinical trials. *Cochrane Database of Methodology Reviews, 3*, Art. No.: MR000011. DOI: 000010.001002/14651858.MR14000011.

Hopewell, S., McDonald, S., Clarke, M., & Egger, M. (2006). Grey literature in meta-analyses of randomized trials of health care interventions. In *The Cochrane Database of Systematic Reviews, 2.* Chichester, UK: John Wiley & Sons.

Hunter, J. E., & Schmidt, F. L. (2004). *Methods of meta-analysis: Correcting error and bias in research findings* (2nd ed.). Newbury Park, CA: SAGE.

Hunter, J. E., Schmidt, F. L., & Hunter, R. (1979). Differential validity of employment tests by race: A comprehensive review and analysis. *Psychological Bulletin, 86*, 721–735.

Ioannidis, J., & Lau, J. (2001). Evolution of treatment effects over time: Empirical insights from recursive cumulative meta-analyses. *Proceedings of the National Academy of Science U S A, 98*, 831–836.

Ioannidis, J. P. A., & Trikalinos, T. A. (2007). The appropriateness of asymmetry tests for publication bias: A large survey. *Canadian Medical Association Journal, 176*(8), 1091–1096.

James, A., Soler, A., & Weatherall, R. (2005). Cognitive behavioural therapy for anxiety disorders in children and adolescents. *Cochrane Database of Systematic Reviews, 4*, Art. No.: CD004690. DOI: 10.1002/14651858.CD004690.pub2.

Jørgensen, A. W., Hilden, J., & Gøtzsche, P. G. (2006). Cochrane reviews compared with industry supported meta-analyses and other meta-analyses of the same drugs: Systematic review. *British Medical Journal, 333*, 782–785.

Jüni, P., Altman, D. G., & Egger, M. (2001). Assessing the quality of controlled clinical trials. *British Medical Journal, 323*, 42–46.

Jüni, P., Witschi, A., Bloch, R., & Egger, M. (1999). The hazards of scoring the quality of clinical trials for meta-analysis. *Journal of the American Medical Association, 282*, 1054–1060.

Kendrick, D., Coupland, C., Mulvaney, C., Simpson, J., Smith, S. J., Sutton, A., et al. (2007). Home safety education and provision of safety equipment for injury prevention. *Cochrane Database of Systematic Reviews, 1*, Art. No.: CD005014. DOI: 10.1002/14651858.CD005014.pub2.

Kunz, R., & Oxman, A. D. (1998). The unpredictability paradox: Review of empirical comparisons of randomised and nonrandomised clinical trials. *British Medical Journal, 317*, 1185–1190.

Larzelere, R. E., Kuhn, B. R., & Johnson, B. (2004). The intervention selection bias: An underrecognized confound in intervention research. *Psychological Bulletin, 130*, 289–303.

Lauver, S. (2002). *Assessing the benefits of an after-school program for urban youth: Results of an experimental design and process evaluation.* Unpublished doctoral dissertation. Philadelphia: University of Pennsylvania.

Leschied, A. W., & Cunningham, A. (2002). *Seeking effective interventions for young offenders: Interim results of a four-year randomized study of Multi-systemic Therapy in Ontario, Canada.* London, Ontario: Centre for Children and Families in the Justice System.

Lexchin, J., Bero, L. A., Djulbegovic, B., & Clark, O. (2003). Pharmaceutical industry sponsorship and research outcome and quality: Systematic review. *British Medical Journal, 326*, 1167–1170.

Light, R. J., & Pillemer, D. B. (1984). *Summing up: The science of reviewing research.* Cambridge, MA: Harvard University Press.

Lipsey, M. W., & Wilson, D. B. (1993). The efficacy of psychological, educational, and behavioral treatment. Confirmation from meta-analysis. *American Psychologist, 48*, 1181–1209.

Lipsey, M. W., & Wilson, D. B. (2001). *Practical meta-analysis.* Thousand Oaks, CA: SAGE Publications.

Littell, J. H. (2005). Lessons from a systematic review of effects of Multisystemic Therapy. *Children and Youth Services Review, 27*, 445–463.

Littell, J. H. (in press). Evidence-based or biased? The quality of published reviews of evidence-based practices. *Children & Youth Services Review.*

Littell, J. H., Campbell, M., Green, S. J., & Toews, B. (2007). Screening and data extraction forms: Systematic review and meta-analysis of effects of Multi-systemic Therapy (MST). Unpublished paper. Bryn Mawr, PA: Bryn Mawr College.

Littell, J. H., Popa, M., & Forsythe, B. (2005). Multisystemic Therapy for social, emotional, and behavioral problems in youth aged 10–17 (Cochrane Review). In: *The Cochrane Database of Systematic Reviews, 4, 2005.* Chichester, UK: John Wiley & Sons. Also available at http://www.campbellcollaboration.org/doc-pdf/Mst_Littell_Review.pdf.

Luborsky, L., Diguer, L., Seligman, D. A., Rosenthal, R., Krause, E. D., Johnson, S., et al. (1999). The researcher's own therapy allegiances: A "wild card" in comparisons of treatment efficacy. *Clinical Psychology: Science and Practice, 6,* 95–106.

Lundahl, B., & Yaffe, J. (2007). Use of meta-analysis in social work and allied disciplines. *Journal of Social Service Research, 33,* 1–11.

Macdonald, G. M., Higgins, J. P. T., & Ramchandani, P. (2006). Cognitive-behavioural interventions for children who have been sexually abused. *Cochrane Database of Systematic Reviews, 4.* Also available at http://www.campbellcollaboration.org/doc-pdf/B9804CAMPBELLFINAL.PDF.

McLeod, B. D., & Weisz, J. R. (2004). Using dissertations to examine potential bias in child and adolescent clinical trials. *Journal of Consulting and Clinical Psychology, 72,* 235–251.

Miller, W., & Wilbourne, P. (2002). Mesa Grande: A methodological analysis of clinical trials of treatments for alcohol use disorders. *Addiction, 97,* 265–277.

Mitchell, O., Wilson, D. B., & MacKenzie, D. L. (2006). The effectiveness of incarceration-based drug treatment on criminal behavior. *The Campbell Collaboration Library.* Retrieved October 10, 2007, from http://www.campbellcollaboration.org/doc-pdf/Incarceration-BasedDrugTxSept06final.pdf.

Moher, D., Cook, D. J., Eastwood, S., Olkin, I., Rennie, D., Stroup, D. F., et al. (1999). Improving the quality of reports of meta-analyses of randomised controlled trials: The QUOROM statement. *The Lancet, 354,* 1896–1900.

Moher, D., Schulz, K., & Altman, D. (2001). The CONSORT statement: Revised recommendations for improving the quality of parallel-group randomized trials. *Annals of Internal Medicine, 134,* 657–662.

Moher, D., Tetzlaff, J., Tricco, A. C., Sampson, M., & Altman, D. G. (2007). Epidemiology and reporting characteristics of systematic reviews. *PLoS Med, 4*(3), e78.

National Health Service Centre for Reviews and Dissemination. (2001). *Undertaking systematic reviews of research on effectiveness* (2nd ed.). York, England: University of York. Available at http://www.york.ac.uk/inst/crd/report4.htm.

Nugent, W. (2006). The comparability of the standardized mean difference effect size across different measures of the same construct. *Educational and Psychological Measurement, 66,* 612–624.

Ogilvie, D., Egan, M., Hamilton, V., & Petticrew, M. (2005). Systematic reviews of health effects of social interventions: Best available evidence: How low should you go? *Journal of Epidemiological Community Health, 59*, 886–892.

Pappadopulos, E., Woolston, S., Chait, A., Perkins, M., Connor, D. F., & Jensen, P. S. (2006). Pharmacotherapy of aggression in children and adolescents: Efficacy and effect size. *Journal of the Canadian Academy of Child and Adolescent Psychiatry, 15*, 27–39.

Patrick, T. B., Demiris, G., Folk, L. C., Moxley, D. E., Mitchell, J. A., & Tao, D. (2004). Evidence-based retrieval in evidence-based medicine. *Journal of the Medical Library Association, 92*, 196–199.

Petrosino, A., Turpin-Petrosino, C., & Buehler, J. (2003). Scared Straight and other juvenile awareness programs for preventing juvenile delinquency (updated Campbell Collaboration review). In *The Campbell Collaboration Library.* Retrieved October 10, 2007, from http://www.campbellcollaboration.org/doc-pdf/ssrupdt.pdf.

Petticrew, M. (2001). Systematic reviews from astronomy to zoology: Myths and misconceptions. *British Medical Journal, 322*, 98–101.

Petticrew, M., & Roberts, H. (2006). *Systematic reviews in the social sciences: A practical guide.* Oxford, UK: Blackwell Publishing.

Ritter, G., Denny, G., Albin, G., Barnett, J., & Blankenship, V. (2006). The effectiveness of volunteer tutoring programs: A systematic review. In *The Campbell Collaboration Library.* Retrieved October 10, 2007, from http://www.campbellcollaboration.org/doc-pdf/Ritter_VolTutor_Rev.pdf.

Rosenthal, R. (1979). The file drawer problem and tolerance of null results. *Psychological Bulletin, 86*, 638–641.

Rosenthal, R., & Rubin, D. B. (1979). Interpersonal expectancy effects: The first 345 studies. *Behavioral and Brain Sciences, 3*, 377–386.

Rosenthal, R., & Rubin, D. B. (1983). A simple, general purpose display of magnitude of experimental effect. *Journal of Educational Psychology, 74*, 166–169.

Rothstein, H., Sutton, A. J., & Bornstein, M. (Eds.). (2005). *Publication bias in meta-analysis: Prevention, assessment, and adjustments.* Chichester, UK: Wiley.

Rothstein, H. R., Turner, H. M., & Lavenberg, J. G. (2004). *The Campbell Collaboration information retrieval policy brief.* Retrieved June 12, 2006, from http://www.campbellcollaboration.org/MG/IRMGPolicyBriefRevised.pdf.

Sackett, D. L. (2000). The sins of expertness and a proposal for redemption. *British Medical Journal, 320*(7244), 1283.

Sackett, D. L., Haynes R. B., Guyatt, G. H., & Tugwell, P. (1991). *Clinical epidemiology: A basic science for clinical medicine* (2nd ed.). Boston: Little, Brown.

Sanchez-Meca, J., Chacon-Moscoso, S., & Marin-Martinez, F. (2003). Effect-size indices for dichotomized outcomes in meta-analysis. *Psychological Methods, 8,* 448–467.

Scher, L. S., Maynard, R. A., & Stagner, M. (2006). Interventions intended to reduce pregnancy-related outcomes among teenagers. In *The Campbell Collaboration Library.* Retrieved October 10, 2007, from http://www.campbell collaboration.org/doc-pdf/teenpregreview__dec2006.pdf.

Scherer, R. W., Langenberg, P., & von Elm, E. (2007). Full publication of results initially presented in abstracts. *Cochrane Database of Systematic Reviews, 2.*

Schultz, K. F., Chalmers, I., Hayes, R. J., & Altman, D. G. (1995). Empirical evidence of bias: Dimensions of methodological quality associated with estimates of treatment effects in controlled trials. *Journal of the American Medical Association, 273,* 408–412.

Schulz, K. F., & Grimes, D. A. (2002). Allocation concealment in randomised trials: Defending against deciphering. *The Lancet, 359,* 614–618.

Shadish, W. R. (1995). The logic of generalization: Five principles common to experiments and ethnographies. *American Journal of Community Psychology, 23,* 419–427.

Shadish, W. R. (2007). A new method for meta-analysis of single-case designs. Presentation at the Second Annual Meeting of the Society for Research Synthesis Methodology, Evanston, IL, July 11, 2007.

Shadish, W. R., Cook, T. D., & Campbell, D. T. (2002). *Experimental and quasi-experimental designs for generalized causal inference.* Boston: Houghton Mifflin.

Shadish, W. R., Matt, G. E., Navarro, A. M. & Phillips, G. (2000). The effects of psychological therapies under clinically representative conditions: A meta-analysis. *Psychological Bulletin, 126,* 512–529.

Shadish, W., & Myers, D. (2004). *Campbell Collaboration research design policy brief.* Retrieved June 12, 2007, from http://www.campbellcollaboration.org/MG/ResDesPolicyBrief.pdf.

Shadish, W. R., & Ragsdale, K. (1996). Random versus nonrandom assignment in controlled experiments: Do you get the same answer? *Journal of Consulting and Clinical Psychology, 64,* 1290–1306.

Shea, B. J., Grimshaw, J. M., Wells, G. A., Boers, M., Andersson, N., Hamel, C., et al. (2007). Development of AMSTAR: A measurement tool to assess the methodological quality of systematic reviews. *BMC Medical Research Methodology, 7.* Available at http://www.biomedcentral.com/1471–2288/7/10.

Shlonsky, A., & Saini, M. (2005). Risk of child maltreatment: A systematic review of the predictive validity of instruments (title registration form). In *The Campbell Collaboration Library.* Retrieved October 10, 2007, from http://www.campbellcollaboration.org/doc-pdf/Shlonsky_Childmaltreat_Title.pdf.

Smedslund, G., Hagen, K. B., Steiro, A., Johme, T., Dalsbø, T. K., & Rud, M. G. (2006). Work programmes for welfare recipients. In *The Campbell Collaboration Library*. Retrieved October 10, 2007, from http://www.campbellcol laboration.org/doc-pdf/Smedslund_Workprog_Review.pdf.

Smith, M. L., & Glass, G. V. (1977). Meta-analysis of psychotherapy outcome studies. *American Psychologist, 32,* 752–760.

Song, F., Eastwood, A. J., Gilbody, S., Duley, L., & Sutton, A. J. (2000). Publication and related biases. *Health Technology Assessment, 4*(10).

Sterne, J. A. C., Becker, B. J., & Egger, M. (2005). The funnel plot. In H. R. Rothstein, A. J. Sutton, & M. Bornstein (Eds.), *Publication bias in meta-analysis: Prevention, assessment and adjustments* (pp. 75–98). West Sussex, UK: John Wiley & Sons.

Sterne, J. A. C., Bradburn, M. J., & Egger, M. (2001). Meta-analysis in Stata^{TM}. In M. Egger, G. Davey Smith, & D. G. Altmann (Eds.), *Systematic reviews in health care: Meta-analysis in context* (pp. 347–369). London, UK: BMJ Publishing Group.

Stone, J., Smyth, R., Carson, A., Lewis, S., Prescott, R., Warlow, C., & Sharpe, M. (2005). Systematic review of misdiagnosis of conversion symptoms and "hysteria." *British Medical Journal, 332,* 989–994.

Stroup, D. F., Berlin, J. A., Morton, S. C., Olkin, I., Williamson, G. D., Rennie, D., et al. (2000). Meta-analysis of observational studies in epidemiology— A proposal for reporting. *Journal of the American Medical Association, 283,* 2008–2012.

Sugarman, D. B., & Hotaling, G. T. (1997). Intimate violence and social desirability: A meta-analytic review. *Journal of Interpersonal Violence, 12,* 275–290.

Sutton, A. J., Abrams, K. R., Jones, D. R., Sheldon, T. A., & Song, F. (1998). Systematic reviews of trials and other studies. *Health Technology Assessment, 2*(19).

Sweeney, L., & Haney, C. (1992). The influence of race on sentencing: a meta-analytic review of experimental studies. *Behavioral Science in Law, 10,* 179–195.

Thompson, D. C., & Rivara, F. P. (1998). Pool fencing for preventing drowning in children. *Cochrane Database of Systematic Reviews, 1,* Art. No.: CD001047. DOI: 10.1002/14651858.CD001047.

Torgerson, C. J. (2006). Publication bias: The Achilles' heel of systematic reviews? *British Journal of Educational Studies, 54,* 89–102.

Trikalinos, T. A., Churchill, R., Ferri, M., Leucht, S., Tuunainen, A., Wahlbeck, K., et al. (2004). Effect sizes in cumulative meta-analyses of mental health randomized trials evolved over time. *Journal of Clinical Epidemiology, 57,* 1124–1130.

Vidanapathirana, J., Abramson, M. J., Forbes, A., & Fairley, C. (2005). Mass media interventions for promoting HIV testing. *Cochrane Database of Systematic Reviews, 3*. Art. No.: CD004775. DOI: 10.1002/14651858.CD004775. pub2.

Videka-Sherman, L. (1988). Meta-analysis of research on social work practice in mental health. *Social Work, 33*, 325–338.

Wang, M. C., & Bushman, B. J. (1999). *Integrating results through meta-analytic review using SAS(R) software.* Cary, NC: SAS Institute.

Wells, K., & Littell, J. H. (manuscript submitted for review). Study quality assessment in systematic reviews of research on intervention effects.

Williamson, P., Altman, D., Gamble, C., Dodd, S., Dwan, K., & Kirkham, J. (2006, February). *Outcome reporting bias in meta-analysis.* Paper presented at the Fourteenth Cochrane Colloquium, Dublin, Ireland.

Williamson, P. R., & Gamble, C. (2005). Identification and impact of outcome selection bias in meta-analysis. *Statistics in Medicine, 24*, 1547–1561.

Wilson, D. B., & Lipsey, M. W. (2001). The role of method in treatment effectiveness research: Evidence from meta-analysis. *Psychological Methods, 6*, 413–429.

Wilson, D. B., MacKenzie, D. L., & Mitchell, F. N. (2005). Effects of correctional boot camps on offending. *The Campbell Collaboration Library.* Retrieved October 10, 2007, from http://www.campbellcollaboration.org/doc-pdf/ Wilson_bootcamps_rev.pdf.

Wilson, S. J., & Lipsey, M. W. (2006a). The effects of school-based social information processing interventions on aggressive behavior: Part I: Universal programs. *The Campbell Collaboration Library.* Retrieved October 10, 2007, from http://www.campbellcollaboration.org/doc-pdf/wilson_socinfoprocuniv_ review.pdf.

Wilson, S. J., & Lipsey, M. W. (2006b). The effects of school-based social information processing interventions on aggressive behavior: Part II: Selected/ indicated pull-out programs. *The Campbell Collaboration Library.* Retrieved October 10, 2007, from http://www.campbellcollaboration.org/doc-pdf/ wilson_socinfoprocpull_review.pdf.

Wilson, S. J., Lipsey, M. W., & Soydan, H. (2003). Are mainstream programs for juvenile delinquency less effective with minority than majority youth? A meta-analysis of outcomes research. *Research on Social Work Practice, 13*, 3–26.

Wortman, P. M. (1994). Judging research quality. In H. Cooper & L. V. Hedges (Eds.), *The handbook of research synthesis* (pp. 97–109). New York: Russell Sage Foundation.

Zaza, S., Briss, P. A., & Harris, K. W. (Eds.) (2005). *The guide to community preventive services: What works to promote health?* New York: Oxford University Press. Chapter 10. Available at http://www.thecommunityguide.org/methods/methods.pdf.

Zief, S. G., Lauver, S., & Maynard, R. A. (2006). Impacts of after-school programs on student outcomes. In *The Campbell Collaboration Library*. Retrieved October 10, 2007, from http://www.campbellcollaboration.org/doc-pdf/zief_afterschool_review.pdf.

Zimbalist, S. E. (1977). *Historic themes and landmarks in social welfare research.* New York: Harper & Row.

Index